This book is for everyone
who is able to create change,
for a better tomorrow.

Monique

Beatnik

First published in 2020 by Beatnik Publishing.

Text: © 2020 Monique Hemmingson
Copy Editor: Laura Tuck

Photographs: © 2020 Erin Cave, with the exception of the
following, pages 38-43 – Sarah Ryland, pages 58-65 – Jono Parker,
pages 98-101 & 104-107 – Alexander Knorr, page 103 – Stefan
Haworth, pages 116-123 – Claudia Smith, pages 174 & 175 –
Maxwell Finch, and page 231 – Bobby Clarke.

Design, Typesetting & Cover: © 2020 Beatnik Publishing
Creative: Sally Greer

Printed and bound in China using plant-based inks on Forest
Stewardship Council® (FSC®)–certified paper and other
controlled material in a BSCI and SEDEX certified workplace.

FSC
www.fsc.org

MIX
Paper from
responsible sources
FSC® C124385

ISBN 978-0-9951180-4-1

www.beatnikpublishing.com

PO Box 8276, Symonds Street,
Auckland 1150, New Zealand

WILD KINSHIP

CONVERSATIONS WITH CONSCIOUS ENTREPRENEURS

MONIQUE HEMMINGSON

Beatnik

CONTENTS

INTRODUCTION

> "Never doubt that a small group of committed citizens have the power to change the world; indeed, it is the only thing that ever has."

– Margaret Mead

Margaret Mead wrote this before the 1980s. Thirty years later I had it tattooed on the inside of my arm, and in the ten years since I've constantly been reminded and re-educated of its unwavering truth, be that in a positive or negative light.

I believe in recent years that many of us have woken to the damage we've done to our land, and by affiliation, our own health and wellbeing. It seems quite obvious to me, when we look back, the ways in which we went wrong, the outcomes that have resulted, and the dangerous space we now find ourselves in. But, to many of us, it can all be quite large, overwhelming, confusing and, frankly, heart-breaking. However, understanding what we can do as an individual appears to be the key to a better future.

I hope that within these pages you and I can find practical ways to become better. I hope that through this we might understand our power as a consumer and how to channel it.

That we can learn the importance and huge impact of consciousness within consumerism and that it doesn't equal sacrifice, but empowerment.

That we can see you be an ordinary person, who chooses to do more. That it's less about perfection and more about prioritising values.

Lastly, I wanted to shine a light, even if only for a moment, on some incredible beings with incredible stories (and in often cases, large sacrifices). These are the people forging a new path and leading in their fields. The people who lie awake at night with busy minds and spend their spare time toiling away to create a positive offering to their communities. They may be big, they may be small, they may be new, they may be old, they may be making a huge mark globally, they may be influencing only their neighbours.

They may not be perfect, but ultimately they're good - and they're changing the world in their wake.

Throughout this journey I was truly overwhelmed by the kind-hearted nature and authenticity of these people who welcomed me into their homes and lives with open arms. Whether it was simply time spent, wisdom and words, energy or gifts, these busy business people were abundant in it and we left with full arms, hearts and minds.

And as I travelled between these people and places, for one reason or another new notions began to wash over me. Words like community, connectivity and togetherness, purpose and creation, generosity and kindness.

I'd set out to give examples of how the world could be changed positively in an environmental sense when we supported these companies and the many like them, but finished my journey feeling as though by doing so, we're embodying a better world through so much more than environmental sustainability alone.

Simply by having an understanding, a connection and taking responsibility of where our products come from, as both a consumer and a supplier, we can enrich and deepen our lives and create physical and emotional wellness, community and a sense of belonging, thereby benefitting the world on a much larger scale.

A dear friend recently said, "The word sustainable is much bigger than we realise. Be it the environment, economy, or in health, they must all work together for a positive force of longevity and holistic nourishment."

Which serves as another example of change upon us, and one I had the honour of seeing firsthand. One where business models and our weekly shopping lists are not only driven by profits and margins, competition and greed, but by community and collaboration, by kindness and nurturing, with mindfulness, honesty, balance, integrity, authenticity and love.

– Monique

THE DAILY BAR
ORGANIC SNACK BARS

AL THURSFIELD

BYRON BAY

How did the The Daily Bar come to be?

It's pretty clichéd, but I've always been really into health and had been on a long health journey personally. I felt like there was a big gap in the market for an honestly healthy snack. We live in such a fast-paced world and so many people don't have time to eat properly, so they're using snacks to get them through the day. I wanted to create a healthier option that was more accessible.

I previously ran a small muesli company with an old friend and had worked in raw food production. I studied environmental science, so it's nice to be bringing that qualification full circle and be working in a field that has the environment at its forefront. The Daily Bar is a combination of all of my past experiences and passions combined. It almost feels like this bar is a catalyst for that.

What did you set out to achieve?

There's a lot of waste behind the scenes and not a lot of quality or transparency out there, particularly in the food industry. I think, as business owners, we should be taking responsibility for the effects our own output and products have on the environment and their lifecycle, with more sustainable closed-loop food production. The Daily Bar makes snacks that are not only sustainable for the planet but also for the consumer. We like to call them nutritionally superior.

We've nearly been running for three years now and have around 150 stockists in Australia, along with our online platform.

Are there any standout hardships you've come across?

There have been so many, big and small, like with any business. But I think a big one was that we tried to run before we could walk and grew too quickly. We were approached to do some collaborations with people and had some export opportunities quite early on, which was all very exciting. But in essence, it ended up taking my attention and energy away from what I really wanted to be doing, which was taking care of my own brand and our market in Australia. We opened ourselves up to being taken advantage of in some areas with our recipes. We were so young and still small as a business - I guess we were a bit naive in trusting people and not covering ourselves.

What have been some key learning experiences?

Someone once told me you want to hire someone who's better than you at each role, which I think is really valuable advice. I'm lucky to have an amazing, albeit small team. We have the same passion and vision but work very much in our own specialised fields, which is a great balance.

> I think, as business owners, we should be taking responsibility for the effects our own output and products have on the environment and their lifecycle.

What's the difference between your production process and that of standard muesli bars on the market?

We worked together with naturopaths and nutritionists to create our products, so they're really high in good fats and fibres, low in artificial sugars and there's no fillers or nasty preservatives. We more or less take a bunch of beautiful, nutritiously dense organic ingredients and smoosh it into a bar. Other natural bars on the market are bound with sugars like dates, whereas we use good fats like coconut butter and tahini instead.

We have our production process down to a pretty fine art now, they're all handmade and hand-packaged but we can make around 2000 bars a day.

Muesli bars in general are a super saturated market and a lot of people early on thought I was crazy to try and compete, but so many of those bars are just the same product with a different name. There's very few that actually have anything good in them at all. They typically have milk powders, colours, flavours and sugar galore, or sometimes you come across a better option but then it has fifteen dates in it. People end up eating their entire day's sugar intake in a single snack bar.

What's the importance of label reading and understanding what's really in our food?

It can be hard because marketing buzzwords are really abused, so words like 'natural' mean absolutely nothing once you read the ingredients. Something that we're struggling with is that it's commercially viable to have a long shelf-life for the products and that's what people want, but food shouldn't, in many cases, be left on the shelf for six plus months. Food is a perishable item at the end of the day. You have to ask yourself, if it can last that long, what's been added to it? Fresh and as close to nature as possible is always going to be best. You should be familiar with every word in your food labels so that your body's familiar, too. Educating yourself and being aware of what you're actually eating is so important, and an easy practice you can take control of in your day-to-day life. You'd be really surprised to find what they put in your standard food items.

Protecting our environment has always been on my radar. Ever since I was a little kid, I've wanted to save the world.

How does The Daily Bar's production aid environmental sustainability?

Our goal is to have a completely closed-loop production cycle. We currently make sure all our food scraps in the kitchen are taken to pigs or composted, we source our honey locally, we're completely plastic free, we use a solar powered carbon neutral printer and vegetable ink on 100 percent recyclable card for our boxes, and the inner wrap is made from a birch fibre so it breaks down in your home compost. Making these little swaps to reduce how much rubbish we're putting out each week, which at the moment is just one small bag, can make a big difference.

We try to capture the whole wellness lifestyle and be really transparent in our production process so people can see it's possible, and actually not that hard. It's also important to me to share information - I understand people keep these business contacts close to heart but I think sharing them so we can all be involved is so much better in the long run.

I don't necessarily think everyone has to be perfect in their environmental crusade, but if everyone is doing it better, or pretty well, then that's going to have a huge effect.

What's the best piece of advice you've been given in regard to small business?

A really close friend of mine who has a super successful business once said to me *"Don't let the bastard get you down"*. When you have a small business, you're so personally invested in everything that you do, and people are just so willing to give you their opinion - especially criticism. But staying true to your vision and goals and what you believe in with every cell in your body really gives you the resilience to deflect other people's negativity and get through the tough times. Small business is hard, so you need to be all in and believe in yourself and your product.

What, in your eyes, is the company's biggest success?

Being able to talk with people and connect through what we're doing and educate them about wellness as a whole. Having a platform where we can empower people and provide better options is what really keeps me going.

What does a better world mean to you?

A simpler world. Where we gain perspective in what really matters in life, our impact on other people and the environment, and by having a sense of accountability. Somewhere along the line we've been distracted, but a better world would be waking up to what that means collectively.

What would be your biggest sacrifice in running The Daily Bar?

I think once you start, it can feel like the work's never done. You're continually inspired to be doing more and more, which makes it hard to switch off. I'm The Daily Bar and The Daily Bar is me, so in ways you lose your identity to it. That, and I would really love a holiday!

What are your biggest passions beyond this?

My biggest passion would be surfing. In studying environmental sciences, protecting our environment has always been on my radar. Ever since I was a little kid, I've wanted to save the world. I think if I wasn't doing this, I'd be doing something in the environmental realm.

Who's your biggest inspiration?

My mum is a really strong, powerful go-getter. I have two older brothers and from a really young age it was drilled into me that anything my brothers did, I could do too. She's been such a source of inspiration, bringing up three kids and never missing a beat while working full-time. I think she really prepared me to be a confident and conscious woman, which is important in the world we're living in.

> I have two older brothers and from a really young age it was drilled into me that anything my brothers did, I could do too.

Do you have any daily rituals?

I always commit to a few hours of me time in the morning. You generally don't finish at five o'clock when you have your own business, but if I've started the day out in the ocean having a surf and being close to nature, then I'm not in such a rush at the end of the day.

Do you meditate?

I've only just started meditating, which I'd been putting off for a long time. I have a really busy mind, which I sometimes see as my biggest asset, but it's good to learn how to slow it down. Generally, though, surfing is my biggest meditation. I can't be angry after a session, it's so grounding.

What does success mean to you?

For The Daily Bar, success is when other people can look to us as an example and see that it's possible to have a financially viable, thriving business that has more values and foundations than just profit.

I'd really like to be able to create a blueprint for other businesses to use so that they can have a closed-loop ethical cycle within their own companies. Personally, being able to maintain a lifestyle like this, that I love, and sharing wellness with people.

In the world of environmental sustainability, what's an innovative company you'd recommend and why?

I really admire Patagonia and what they do. Being able to achieve such a global reach is incredible. It inspires small businesses like me to see that it's possible to have environmental sustainability at the core of your business and on such a huge scale.

Where do you hope to be five years from now?

I'd really love if The Daily Bar was more than just a snack bar - a whole food range where people could trust they were getting that same quality - would be amazing.

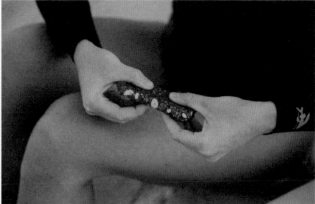

I don't necessarily think everyone has to be perfect in their environmental crusade, but if everyone is doing it better, or pretty well, then that's going to have a huge effect.

COUNTRY KITCHEN
BOTANICAL SKINCARE

HANNAH JACK

KAUKAPAKAPA

How did Country Kitchen come to be?

I grew up on land and with vegetable gardens. My first product was dried flower petals for a whole foods café in Auckland, which was four years ago now. After the success of this first product, I started moving more into flowers. I remember I was op shopping quite a lot at the time and found these old books about herbal remedies and traditional ways of healing, then before I knew it, I had no vegetables and my garden was overrun with flowers and herbs. I find it really funny and beautiful how life takes us on these journeys and certain things just blossom from one moment. From there, I started making kombucha and my second product (which was the calendula-infused balms) and that was it, I was obsessed. I wasn't brought up doing anything like this specifically - I'm completely self-taught.

Were there any standout hardships?

I think a huge one for me is self-doubt. We get so caught up with what everyone else is doing now because of social media, so it's hard not to compare yourself. But you have to look inwards in those times of doubt and understand there has to be ups and downs.

You're allowed to go off the road along the way. And you will.

I think the beginning can also be really hard. I started Country Kitchen with no money and with young kids. I found that 'work mum life' to be really challenging and something that's constantly evolving.

A good lesson that brings me comfort is that every single person is unique - even if someone's doing what you're doing, it will never be the same as you. Everyone has a different method, so the imprint is different. Once you understand this, things like

fear of competition start to drop away and you bloom. It can be a hard thing to arrive at, but it really is true. And you know you can go off this road a thousand times - there's always going to be uncertainty when you're finding your path - but once you find it, oh it's amazing! You're allowed to go off the road along the way. And you will.

Life takes us on these journeys and certain things just blossom from one moment.

What have been some key learning experiences?

People often ask what courses I took or ask me where to start. I always say the garden is my biggest inspiration. When you're working with plants, especially within the alchemy and healing side, nature and the seasons tell you so much. Even if you wanted to study in the future, the best thing you can do is start building your own foundations first and be out in the garden experiencing what it has to offer and start living it. The plants tell you when they're ready, when they're best for you or when you're meant to be having them, thanks to seasons. Nature literally shows us everything, we just need to learn to listen. It slows you down considerably and teaches you a lot of patience.

I also found when you start a business you actually learn a lot about yourself and your strengths and weaknesses, and oh my gosh, it can be confronting. You need to know your weaknesses though so you can catch them, start working on them or find other ways, like getting staff whose strengths cover your weaknesses.

What's the difference between your products and regular skincare on the market?

Regular skincare, like what you'd find at the supermarket for example, it's white, it's watery, you put it on your face and feel like you need to constantly reapply it. My products are really thick, creamy and have a lot of colour. I work with oils like bright orange calendula oil and rich honeyed bees wax, hydrosols and plant's spirit which makes it a very different product. It also makes you wonder how these other creams became white. I liken the method to how we eat; I make everything from scratch because what you make with your own hands is so good for you and your family, especially in the way of energy. The quote *"You can bake one recipe one day in a good mood and it will turn out so differently if you bake it in a bad mood"* refers to that energy and intention behind the task. Here in the studio, I take that really seriously and if I'm feeling a bit off then I won't make anything. I get all these emails from people saying when they use my product, they can really feel the difference and feel what's gone into it. That's my integrity and what I strive for. So, really, the differences between the products are endless.

In my workshops, we start by picking plants straight from the garden and then we infuse the oils. As we go through the stages people are just mind boggled. It's such an eye opener. There's so much work that goes into these products and you can feel that when you use them.

What, in your words, is the importance of chemical-free skincare?

Your skin is your largest organ. It's your environment externally, just as it is internally, so it's really important and just as sensitive. We think of our skin as such a hardy thing, but it isn't. Everything you put on your skin, you should be able to eat (and vice-versa). A connection with your skin is also really important, so I oil my body every night. Your skin will tell you everything that's going on within your body - you can read people through their eyes or their tongue, just like through their skin. So, when something's going on with our skin like eczema, acne or dermatitis, it's our body's messenger telling us that there's something wrong internally. We should never ever suppress a symptom, we should only ever dig deeper.

The farm is a really sacred place for you, can you tell us more about it?

We're based in Kaukapakapa which is a really beautiful place and I aim to be very invested in this community. I consciously don't travel out of Kaukapakapa through the week. Staying in your community is really important.

Living out here is an embodiment of a whole lifestyle, it's not just about the business, but food and pace and mindfulness, too.

I work off an organic and sustainable traditional homestead practice. We eat our own homekill and

lots of vegetables from our garden. If we can't grow or source something locally, we generally won't eat it. We don't really grow or eat wheat, almonds or soybeans for example, so we grow our own beans and we milk our goats instead.

I want to be able to look at my plate and know exactly where everything has come from. I raised this meat, my chickens laid those eggs, I nurtured those vegetables. In regard to our homekill, we raise them, we love them, we respect their death and it's a really important lesson, especially for the kids. We have a few goats, cows, sheep, pigs, horses and chickens and when we walk down the farm the animals trail after us. They love us. They really are like children with their little routines and different personalities.

We should never ever suppress a symptom, we should only ever dig deeper.

How does the production of the farm aid environmental sustainability?

We're completely spray-free here on the farm and use traditional homestead methods throughout. Everything is circular, from the chickens to the horse manure. We eat everything grown in the garden and our scraps go in the compost or to the pigs. Very little plastic and waste leaves this property, I guess not a lot comes on either because we largely live off the land. I'm really fortunate to have this land, not everyone can have that. For those who don't, the best thing they can do is support their local farmers. Go to the farmers' market and take advantage of the goodness people are offering. They put so much work into it, it really is their life and your support is everything. It enables them to continue forward.

How do you find work life balance with a young family?

We have a seven and four-year-old, so I found this balance quite hard for a while. I grew up with a stay-at-home mum and that lifestyle for my own children was always really important to me, I wanted to imprint my values and morals on them and give them a life here on the farm - although not putting them in care or giving them a cellphone or TV to

watch all the time was really hard when I was trying to work. That's why I set up the studio in our garage here, so I'm close. My promise to my children is that I'll stay close to home and not move too fast with the business until they're both in school. You have to find a way that works for you and your partner, to put down those foundations and then really stick to them.

What does a better world mean to you?

A connected world, with communities who work together not against each other, and not for things. I love the idea of trade rather than monetary gain. I love tapping into your community's strengths and using one another's resources. That's why I love my workshops. Sharing that knowledge and passion with others is really special and what it's all about.

You have to look inwards in those times of doubt and understand there has to be ups and downs.

What would be your biggest sacrifice in running Country Kitchen?

Honestly, I don't feel like there's anything in the larger scheme of things. I'm just so happy creating and sharing what I am. I guess, if anything, it would be understanding that you can spread yourself across everything thinly, or you can choose to do a couple of things really well. For the moment, it's my family and my work. So, friendships and a social life have definitely dropped off in that process, which has been hard at times.

What's your go-to when you're in a creative rut?

I read, which is actually new for me. I didn't grow up reading a lot. We were much more practical on the farm as children, but now I'm addicted. It's really soul soothing. Whipping my shoes off and going for a walk is also a great way to reconnect and is something I try to do daily.

Who's your biggest inspiration?

The land is my biggest inspiration, always. But if it were a person, Susan Weed is an amazing herbalist who works largely with the circular rhythms of life and has such a wealth of knowledge.

Do you live by a mantra?

Just start by doing. Plant a seed and see where it takes you.

What does success mean to you?

Success, to me, is what I teach my children. I think you're successful in life if you wake up in the morning and are so internally grateful and happy. It can be hard in this world we're living in, there's so much noise now, so much distraction. But it's such a deep, wonderful feeling when you get there.

In the world of environmental sustainability, what's an innovative company you'd recommend and why?

I really love what the bulk stores are doing, places like GoodFor are amazing. These innovative companies are making a difference in a small way but have such a huge ripple effect. I really take my hat off to them. It's such a great place for people to start with something they consume every day, like food.

Where do you hope to be five years from now?

With massive gardens. My life will be The Secret Garden one day with food forests everywhere and workshops and education. It will be a lot of hands on work to get there, but that's where I see myself.

FOLK CAFÉ

MAGGIE +
JULIAN DYLAN

BYRON BAY

How did Folk come to be?

Julian: We're both from art and music backgrounds and had worked in hospitality a bunch in the past, hospitality had always been there for us as a reliable income. An interest in food and coffee grew into a real passion over the years and Folk was an opportunity to bring our love for food, design and music together.

Maggie: We have always really enjoyed making food and throwing dinner parties for our friends. We grew up in the country, but had been living in the city (Melbourne) and were pretty keen to get back to the trees. We played with the idea of packing up the van and further exploring Australia, but after stumbling on this little lease available it just felt perfect, so we decided to embark on a creative project instead. I quite naively thought it would be a little interim project while we had a break from the city and our respective careers, but then it really took off.

When we came upon the building Folk is now in, it was a pretty rough old shack with a cracker dust 'lawn' and steel grates over the windows. We were super broke and negotiated a one-year lease for the first term in case it didn't work out. Then we really just jumped in and tried to be playful, with our limited skills and finances.

If you try to appeal to everyone, then you're appealing to no one.

How has the company grown?

Maggie: Byron Bay was very different back then; still a small coastal town, and very seasonal. There wasn't much of a contemporary café culture.

It was long before the 'wellness' trend really caught on, or even before the term 'plant-based' became a

household phrase. It was pretty fringe. When people realised what we were going to be doing at Folk, both with the concept for the renovations and the concept for the food, they thought we were crazy. We had people knocking on the door while we were building and painting saying, *"Don't do it, it definitely won't work, put in a deep fryer, you have to sell pies"* etc. One guy told us a story how, *"The old owners put on a sausage sizzle out the front over summer and absolutely killed it, why don't you just do that?"* and was very shocked when we said we wouldn't be serving any meat at all. People were really concerned that we didn't know what we were doing. Or frightened for the level change, or both, I'm unsure. It was both humorous and concerning, we'd really thrown our all into this, but it also really highlighted how much it was needed. It is funny to think now that people wouldn't even bat an eyelid at the concept.

You expanded to a new site, Woods [although recently sold] in your second year. How was that experience?

Woods was intended as an extension of Folk, really. We weren't looking to open another business but the opportunity felt too appealing to miss. The development in Bangalow was a beautiful project to be a part of, set next to the Byron Art School and amongst a collection of art studios. It really fit our ethos.

Were there any standout hardships?

Julian: It's been wildly positive and yet so challenging. We feel like we've been through and grown so much in such a short space of time. We didn't have previous business experience so we had to pick this up on the fly. I would say that in my experience managing people is one of the hardest aspects of running a business.

Maggie: Staffing can be really difficult. Suddenly we were managing thirty staff between the two places, many of whom were older than us and with more experience in the field, which was a challenging dynamic. It was a massive learning curve for me in recognising you have a role as an employer, and that you need to constantly maintain your vision, and can't just all be mates. That was hard.

What have been some key learning experience?

Julian: Managing people. People have experiences, belief systems and values different from each other and from our own. The key and the challenge is to create a team where these align. I feel as though I have experienced nearly everything under the sun for a small coffee shop business so I'm no longer surprised as much when the unexpected arrives. When hardships come up, you figure out how to get through it. You're not as shaken and you just solider on.

Maggie: Overall, the business venture has been great from the outset. We had so many people tell us the concept wouldn't work. It has worked, it continues to work, and we've been able to afford that without compromising our values. We feel like the little engine that could.

> Our goal is to introduce people to the idea that you can eat and do business in an ethical way, successfully.

How would you best summarise your offering?

Julian: Specifically, it's a plant-based café, but really my point of view is that it's all about giving people a special experience with exceptional service and nourishing food.

Maggie: We're particular about everything on the same level; food, coffee, atmosphere, service, music, values. Holistically, we are into experiential design. We don't want Folk to be any typical café, we want it to reflect an idealist fantasy, to play out like a film set.

How do Folk's production methods aid environmental sustainability?

Julian: Folk is an extension of us and how we live day-to-day. For example, in our home we'll buy from local and organic growers at farmers' markets and support small businesses whose ethics align with ours.

Obviously, a big one at Folk is that there's no meat on the menu, which of course has a big environmental impact. When you're feeding thousands of people a week without meat, it carries some weight. You could pretty much pick any area of the café and we could tell you how we've chosen to use a more

sustainable option. We feel that we're showing how you can enjoy better quality food that aligns with good ethics as well as creating important awareness around environmental sustainability.

What, in your words, is the importance of eating organic and plant-based?

Maggie: It's well established how eating this way is better for your health, and the vast negative impact animal agriculture has on our environment. And that's without mentioning the ethical aspect, which goes without saying. It is difficult, I have learnt that you need to draw the line somewhere, especially in business, or else you may struggle to stay afloat. Or at least I'm currently exploring this concept. I think understanding 'plant-based' has it's own importance too. Which is more of a diet than a 'lifestyle'. We have been the target of negativity when people feel conflicted that our café isn't vegan. We serve eggs and dairy, albeit very carefully and ethically sourced from local suppliers. But the bottom line is, ethics are subjective. You only have to open your eyes to see how the dairy industry is devastating. The egg industry is devastating. The world is devastating, and what can you do about it? You can opt out, or you can try to be part of positive change. I think they both have merit. We have chosen to serve plant-based food, which is how we eat at home. This is authentic to us, and allows us to remain approachable for a wider audience. We do hope that what we are doing is part of a broader change.

Julian: I think of equal importance too, is the scale and method of production. Everything is hand-crafted on site, so we're not buying in pre-made packaged goods. It's really rare in this industry, to have everything made from scratch. Which obviously cuts down on a lot of packaging and waste and preservatives, and gives us full control over each item. Our goal is to introduce people to the idea that you can eat and do business in an ethical way, successfully.

What advice would you give someone looking to own an ethical small business?

Maggie: Authenticity is key to success. Stay true and be willing to work creatively and persevere. Having an understanding of how much you'll need to work is important too - you do have to give yourself over to it. We've given 100 percent of ourselves to Folk.

Julian: I think if people can find something

they're passionate about and really stick to it and stay true to themselves and their goals, they'll succeed. This goes back to what Maggie said about authenticity. If you try to appeal to everyone, then you're appealing to no one. Learn some business fundamentals, of course, but don't get hung up on those sorts of things. Just find something that you're going to jump out of bed for each day. If you're going to open a small business, you need to be fully invested emotionally for it to work.

What, in your words, is the importance of community?

Julian: Your community is the lifeblood of you continuing to do what you do. If you don't have its support and backing, you can't continue to provide your service, which is essential to be economically sustainable long-term.

> You only have to open your eyes to see how the dairy industry is devastating. The egg industry is devastating. The world is devastating, and what can you do about it? You can opt out, or you can try to be part of positive change.

Maggie: You can't do it without your community. You have to create that community around you, and you need to have a lot of intention with that. Your community isn't just the people physically around you, but the people who choose to be, because of what you offer. These are the people who will support your creation.

Julian: Which really goes back to that authenticity again - small business is hard and so people choose the easy option and do what's common. People like bacon and egg rolls, so that's the easy option. It can be conflicting to go against that and do what no one is doing but finding your niche and point of difference is what creates a community who'll stand by you for the long haul.

What, to you, is the company's biggest success?

Julian: Doing something successfully that goes against the grain and contributes positively to the community and the environment. Putting something like Folk into the world - I think that's pretty cool.

What does a better world mean to you?

Maggie: I want to say authenticity (ha ha) - I know I'm repeating it, but it really is key. Authenticity, compassion, earnestness.

What would be your biggest sacrifice in running a small business?

Julian: You kind of replace the life you once knew for this new life as a small business owner and everything that entails. It's not a sacrifice but a change of life.

What are your biggest passions beyond Folk?

Maggie: Living well, which encompass how you express yourself creatively, what you eat and how you spend your time, having an ethos to how you live. If we weren't working with Folk, we'd be doing something else that allows us to work with these values in the same way. It could manifest in many forms, but would have this same backbone.

Who's your biggest inspiration?

Julian: Each other.

Maggie: (Ha ha) That is dreadfully clichéd. We're in such a bubble. We're either at home or work, all the time together, so we do grow from each other. Julian is my inspiration, he's amazing. But everyone who's an artist, who lives with bravery and carves out their own path is inspiring to me.

Julian: We're also big readers, every book on our shelf is probably someone who we were inspired by.

Do you have any daily rituals?

Julian: Not really, every day is pretty different. We lack structure really.

Maggie: If anything, it probably revolves around food and coffee. Good music. Our dog.

Julian: Feeding our sourdough starter every day, that's probably the most consistent thing in my life right now.

What's your go-to when you're in a creative rut?

Julian: I don't really believe in creative ruts, I guess you can become uninspired or unmotivated but usually I just force myself to start doing again and I find that helps.

Maggie: I think a creative rut is actually more of an emotional rut. We're all creative all the time, but sometimes emotionally we're not in balance so we can struggle to feel motivated.

What does success mean to you?

Julian: It can be different at any one point in time depending on what our values and goals are then. At the moment we really value time, family and space for each other, so if we're achieving that we'll feel successful. It's also easy to take our relationship for granted and I guess that connection on its own is a success.

Maggie: I'm not sure what I really define as success, but I think I feel successful. I feel successful in our love for each other, to love I think is true success. I recently read *"The man said that he would rather live a significant life, than a successful one"*. That feels true to me.

Where do you hope to be five years from now?

Maggie: We have no idea; we had no idea we'd be here five years ago.

Julian: We'll just see where life takes us. Right now, we don't know what we're doing next week!

> I'm not sure what I really define as success, but I think I feel successful. I feel successful in our love for each other, to love I think is true success.

KAMI & KINDRED
CERAMICS

HAYLEY RICHARDS

NELSON

How did Kami & Kindred come to be?

I've always loved ceramics, having special viewing pieces around the house along with functional pieces I use daily. I took a local pottery class about seven years ago. I had an idea in mind for a necklace that I wanted and ended up spending the whole eight-week course making it. After that, I dabbled in clay on my own by making myself some earrings. Strangers often stopped me and asked where my earrings were from and if I could make them a pair. It was really just word of mouth orders for a while until a friend said to me, *"Why don't you set up an online store and start doing this full time?"*

At the time, I'd been running my wellness blog called Gather Girl for around four years, which was the catalyst for many other business ventures and whole food products, and I was practising part-time as a nutritionist between full-time mothering. I was super passionate about the industry, but over time it began to wear on me, and I felt I needed a change to look after my own health. So, some friends and I took a few photos of my ceramics and put them online, and it really took off.

How has the company grown?

I launched my first collection online in 2017, so it's grown a lot and quite quickly since then, especially once I added homewares to my range. Now I stock about thirty stores across New Zealand, Australia and the US, as well as my online store. I never really envisaged the wholesale side being so big and having the reach it does. I knew, and still feel, that it's really important I personally make everything with my own hands and not commission work out, so I need to be careful about where my products are going to ensure I'm able to keep up with demand.

From a business perspective, online sales are my bread and butter. Wholesaling acts as more of an advertising strategy, but it's a lot harder to make money through wholesale. Because of this, I'm really

particular about the places I do stock; most of them are really small businesses that have the same philosophy and ethos in slow and conscious creations, and I'm really honoured to be showcased within their stores and have that worldwide connection.

Are there any standout hardships?

For me, it's missing out on some things in my family life because I'm working. I really struggled with that and felt guilty for a period. Now, I'm really proud that I'm a hardworking mother and my children can see me as an independent, strong woman in both areas of my life. I'm not apologetic for that anymore. But the family thing is definitely the hardest.

Finances can be a tough point too and I think anyone in small business would be able to relate to that, but as long as you do what you love and love what you do, then it's OK. Because it's really not about the money, it's about fulfilment. That's the important part.

What have been some key learning experiences?

Working with clay has taught me not to be attached to material things. Everything is impermanent. I can open a kiln one day and the whole lot can be ruined and needs to be thrown away. You can pour so much work into something and do everything right, but at the end of the day, it's in the hands of the kiln gods and you just have to accept that you're not in control - and that's OK.

Another really big thing was that although I've always loved good quality things, being someone who now fully understands the amount of time, love, passion and energy that goes into a product makes you fully understand the true value in quality items. Without someone appreciating that and paying for it, you couldn't afford to continue to create those beautiful things for the world.

> When I think of slow fashion I think of longevity, quality and mindfulness. It's so imperative that we start being those slow consumers in everything that we do.

What's the difference between your products and other ceramics and jewellery on the market?

Obviously one of the biggest things is that I am Kami & Kindred, and everything is, and will always be, made by me. My jewellery is all hand-built and homewares are all hand-thrown on a wheel. After they're thrown or sculpted, they go into the kiln for their first fire. I then glaze each piece - both stages taking a few days each - before they go back into the kiln.

With the jewellery, I source pure sterling silver from New Zealand companies. The tassels are all naturally hand-dyed and the yarn is ethically and mindfully hand-picked from Japan. My father and I made an old school rope-making machine which I use for my necklaces. It can be a long process - a cup takes a few weeks to complete. A pair of tassel earrings, after the process of the kiln firings and glazing, also takes a few weeks before they're complete. It really is an all-consuming, albeit meditative and beautiful, process.

The coolest thing about my jewellery that sets it apart from other products is that it's so distinctively Kami & Kindred. I try to keep away from trends and focus deeply on what's uniquely me to ensure everything is made with intent and energy. I think that quality is really evident to people when they touch and use my products.

In your words, what does slow fashion mean?

When I think of slow fashion I think of longevity, quality and mindfulness. It's so imperative that we start being those slow consumers in everything that we do.

How does your production method aid environmental sustainability?

The main thing would be that everything I use comes from the earth. It's all sustainable and renewable, from the clay to the dyes to the string and packaging, and that's something I'll never compromise on.

How do you find the work life balance with a young family?

I have three girls. Over time, I realised the invaluable lessons my girls were learning from me, and the guilt of my workload started to slip away. They're learning the value of money and craft. They're very aware of the process of how I make money for our family. It's made them, as children, more mindful about purchases and the value of products.

One thing I always try to do is be really present in whichever task I'm doing, with both my mind and body. If it's with the girls, I'm all there - not on my phone or computer half working. Then when I'm in my studio, I'm fully there, too. Pottery takes all of me and an entirely new energy to anything I've ever done before. I know that if I'm not in the right space and concentrating on my art, I won't get the results.

Working with clay has taught me not to be attached to material things. Everything is impermanent.

What does a better world mean to you?

It would have more conscious consumers and self-love with less comparison. More live time, less screen time. I think the world would be a better place if we could bring back that real community vibe with an it takes a tribe mentality. A lot of that has been lost, but being able to call on your friends and having that support system and interconnectedness around us is huge.

Who's your biggest inspiration?

My children, they've taught me so much. I love watching them and seeing how empathetic and resourceful they are. They've changed who I am as a person and made me so much more conscious and present.

Do you live by a mantra?

Love what you do and do what you love, and I love the quote *"When you're on fire, people come to watch you burn."* Both of these inspire me to stay true to myself and my craft, to listen to my instincts and continue to create.

Do you have any daily rituals?

Rituals are really important - they ground me and give me a sense of security. My biggest one would be setting my intentions in bed in the morning with my fiancé by my side and an almond milk flat white, in a cup that I've made with my own hands. Then the kids will come and jump on the bed and snuggle in. It may be simple, but it really helps me to start my day filled with love and perspective, rather than on a screen or with busyness.

What does success mean to you?

I feel successful now. To me, success is being able to wake up and do what you love every day and having that freedom to live life on your own time. When I want to work, I do. But if I need or want a day out of the studio, I can do that too. It really helps to nurture your love for your work when it's on your terms.

In the world of environmental sustainability, what's an innovative company you'd recommend and why?

I really love what Geami WrapPak by Ranpack does. It's a honeycomb wrap that completely replaces bubble wrap, tissue paper and cardboard. In my industry, shipping big wholesale orders all over the world means you need some seriously good packaging and I love that I can stay true to my values by using their products.

Where do you hope to be five years from now?

Travelling more, and I'd love to see a little Kami & Kindred homeware store somewhere. But nothing too different, I really love where I am right now.

I'm really proud that I'm a hardworking mother and my children can see me as an independent, strong woman in both areas of my life. I'm not apologetic for that anymore.

organic
coffee
roasters

KŌKAKO
COFFEE ROASTERY

MIKE MURPHY

AUCKLAND

How did your past contribute to Kōkako?

When I was seventeen, I got my first job as a pizza delivery boy. I had an amazing boss and over time worked my way up through the ranks to managing the stores. I was with this company right through university and it really threw me into the world of hospitality.

I did a Bachelor of Arts, studying topics like social geography, anthropology, the Pacific Islands and coastal erosion, never really thinking that I'd end up using this knowledge in my future career. After graduation, I stayed with hospitality and ended up working as an area manager for Eagle Boys Pizza. I was working with franchisees to set up and manage their stores, so from quite a young age I learnt how to read profit and loss statements, understand food and labour costs and all of those fundamentals to running a successful business.

In my early twenties I went to London and worked in hospitality recruitment, which was a really different side of the industry again but invaluable learning. When I came back home, I helped to open Auckland's first Hell Pizza and managed that before opening my own one in Botany, East Auckland. It was a really big success and I was immensely proud of what I'd achieved. In time, I sold and moved to Melbourne and worked as a retail food consultant where I worked between our Melbourne and Dubai offices.

How did Kōkako, as we know it, come to be?

During my time in Melbourne I'd often find myself scouring the city for specialty, independent coffee shops. The industry was just starting to take off with the third wave of coffee being established. They were roasting their own beans and had these beautiful fit-outs in restored factories. I used to draw pictures and write down what I noticed. After a while, I decided to head back to New Zealand and do that in Auckland. Eventually, after a lot of market research, I bought Kōkako in May 2007 and since then the brand has been a bit of a chameleon within hospitality. We've been a food and beverage

company, catering business, two cafés, pop-up shop and a coffee roastery. It's been quite the journey.

When I purchased Kōkako there were about 120 coffee roasters within New Zealand, and now there would be well over 300, so the industry has grown a lot.

Are there any standout hardships you've come across?

There have been lots over the years, of course. I'm not sure I really expected to be in it for this long. Starting out, I was overly ambitious. I was trying to build this company of scale with commercial kitchens and cafés, without the financial backing to really do so. I was being a generalist instead of a specialist, which is something in hindsight I would've changed if I could go back. Then the recession hit in 2008, and that was really challenging. It was a pretty tough time. I managed to sell my Parnell café in 2010 which helped to float me through that economic crisis, but I didn't make a profit for about seven years due to that and a lack of strategic planning.

I definitely don't recommend that sort of output without financial gain and proper support. It was a long time and came at the cost of relationships and physical and emotional health. You really give all of yourself to an industry like hospitality and it can be detrimental to other areas of your life.

> I think, in time, things like the single use coffee cup will become like a cigarette, something that's seen as undesirable to be seen walking down the street with.

What advice would you have for someone in business?

I think collaboration is really important in business and in sustainability. Really early on I worked to become Fairtrade and organic certified and joined the Sustainable Business Network. We also worked hard on 'outside the box' methods and did marketing activations and collaborations for small events. We got our name out there like that rather than with big billboards. We're a grassroots organisation and really bootstrapped; we never had a big bankroll to work with so had to grow organically and slowly, which there can be a lot of merit in.

What, to you, is the company's biggest success?

There are many things I'm really proud of within Kōkako; we've stuck to our values and never compromised. Over the years, so many people (especially in the tough times) told me to drop Fairtrade and organics but we were always really resolute about that and never faltered. I'm also really proud of our transparency as a company within sustainability and our two sustainability reports. We've shown a lot of leadership in promoting sustainability alongside coffee. Our relationship with coffee producers in Papua New Guinea has also helped to put their coffee on the map. In the twelve years I've had the business, I've had over 400 employees, which is a huge amount of people to affect and empower. It's been great to see the development of team members over the years, many of whom have gone on to own their own businesses.

> # A better world is one where human beings have a greater awareness of how we can live in a considered and less impactful way. One in which people realise we're living in a circular economy and that we need to be regenerative.

In your words, why is Fairtrade important?

I see Fairtrade as an empowerment tool that's about a hand-up, not a handout. It's about ensuring producer groups and coffee farmers work collaboratively in a democratically elected cooperative structure to ensure they can collectively sell their coffee for a minimum price guarantee. It's about the tools and resources that the Fairtrade system provides on the ground from pest control to improvement in soil quality. And it works to ensure the Fairtrade premium they get goes back into projects that fairly benefit their community, like water sanitation initiatives or building a new school. As a company, we want to see that the Fairtrade premium is being spent properly so we go on origin trips to immerse ourselves in their culture and check that it's been validated, which is really important.

In your words, why are organics important?

Chris Morrison, who's one of our shareholders and the co-founder of Karma Cola and All Good Organics, has taught me a lot about the importance of organics over the years. The bottom line is healthy soil, equals healthy food, equals healthy people. I don't think enough people really understand the importance of healthy soil and how much we've lost. Over time, I've become more personally passionate about organics and have made sure there's continuity between my work and personal life in that regard. I take pride in how little landfill my household produces, composting and buying organic food where possible.

Can you explain how Kōkako works to offset carbon emissions?

It can be quite hard to understand the logistics of carbon offsets and why it's important which is why we developed our sustainability reports. But the bottom line is we should be trying as best we can to exist personally and professionally in a way that doesn't rely on fossil fuels. As a company, this means understanding how we can work with coffee farmers to offset our carbon footprint. We worked with Fairtrade to refine a tool that works out what the emissions are on every kilo of coffee we roast. We get invoiced from Fairtrade for carbon credits which go to Ethiopia to pay for cooking stoves, so they don't need to chop trees down for cooking or heating. It's a good start, it's not perfect, but I believe as an organisation you have to start somewhere towards aiding a better, more regenerative circular economy.

What does a better world mean to you?

A better world is one where human beings have a greater awareness of how we can live in a considered and less impactful way. One in which people realise we're living in a circular economy and that we need to be regenerative. For example, I often go and get sushi for lunch and I'm often the only one who orders it to eat in on a tray. There are countless people every day that come in, purchase a plastic container filled with sushi and sit down for ten minutes to eat the contents before throwing the packaging away. I sit there and watch them and think *this is so fucked*. How did it come to this? We've become so blind to our actions as a society. .

What would be your biggest sacrifice in running a small business?

For me the biggest sacrifice would be not creating enough time or space for myself personally throughout the time I've owned Kōkako. Any business owner will probably agree that it can be all encompassing and this often comes at the sacrifice of things like buying houses, relationships and health. That's quite a big deal and sometimes these sacrifices don't sit that well.

What are your biggest passions beyond Kōkako?

I'm really into architecture. I've built a house in the bush on a section I purchased a few years ago in the Kaipara Habour with my KiwiSaver because Auckland was too expensive. It's very modest - two bedroom, 108sqm - and looks out over the water. Over the years its location and size have become a much-loved element. I love design and things that have a utilitarian function. I'm naturally an introvert, so the idea of having this little sanctuary in the bush works well.

Who's your biggest inspiration?

I've been really inspired by my business partner, Chris Morrison. He's a pioneer in the New Zealand organic sector and has had a long successful career where he's really stuck to his values. From starting and then selling Phoenix Organics, to starting up companies like Karma Cola and then investing in others like Kōkako, what he's done is huge and really admirable. I also admire Jacob and Georgia Faull from Nature Baby; they're super progressive and are so true to their brand. They're not in it just to drive profit and I think that's really important.

What does success mean to you?

I think success is being aware of the positive influence you're having on others, be that personally or professionally. For me, it's less about building a company to a certain stage and more about the people you positively impact or inspire along the way and the impact and influence you achieve in your industry.

In the world of environmental sustainability, what's an innovative company you'd recommend?

I think what Ben Bell from Hungry Bin Worm Farms is doing is really cool – he's creating something environmentally friendly for residential and commercial use that reduces landfill with a design element that makes it desirable to use.

Where do you hope to be five years from now?

I currently do quite a lot of business consulting with like-minded sustainable companies. I like the idea that in the future I can take everything I've learnt from Kōkako and the networks I've built and use them for the greater good. Where in the world I'm not sure, but I think that I can create greater impact beyond Kōkako one day.

> I don't think people are conscious of the decisions they're making. Often our mindset is about getting through life as an individual; getting the kids to school, paying the bills, etc, so we need to empower and educate ourselves to think about what impact our choices now for the next generation.

THE SECRET KITCHEN
AUTHOR + NATUROPATH

JANA BRUNCLIKOVA

SYDNEY

How did your upbringing contribute to The Secret Kitchen?

The Secret Kitchen and naturopathy were both natural developments for me. When I was little, I was always in the kitchen cooking with my mother or collecting herbs at home in the Czech Republic. I grew up outside a lot, living in the mountains, and my grandmother was always making herbal concoctions - so this life has been ingrained in me. I grew up during communism and didn't have a lot of money, so we lived off our gardens because we had to. When communism ended, there were all of these new products on offer; I remember the apples were very shiny, and as a child, I didn't want the fruit from our gardens anymore. I wanted the pretty shiny ones. It's only now that the Czech Republic is starting to return to the mountains and nature, becoming aware again of its roots and the importance of nurturing and living off the land. It was lost for a long time.

> It's only now that the Czech Republic is starting to return to the mountains and nature, becoming aware again of its roots and the importance of nurturing and living off the land. It was lost for a long time.

How did The Secret Kitchen come to be?

I decided to leave Czech because it didn't offer a degree in naturopathy, so I went to the UK to learn English for two years and then to Australia to do my degree. I've now been here for fifteen years and have been practising naturopathy for eleven.

The Secret Kitchen started seven years ago as a passion project. It was a way for me to combine my love of naturopathy, cooking, botanicals, community, adventures and travel. I love showing people how to use plants and nature in cooking and still love to sell my plant-based Earth Cakes.

Can you tell us about your work in naturopathy?

I work in clinic full-time between Orchard St.'s Bronte Clinic and Nimbus & Co. in Byron Bay. I work as a naturopath, herbalist and nutritionist, and offer a little bit of homeopathy along with a Russian practice that uses bio-resonance software called Metatron. I also have a little dispensary at home.

You work across a large range of practices, can you explain this method?

I use bio-resonance as a diagnostic tool. It works on your body's frequencies and vibrations, much like acupuncture. By scanning the body with this machine, I get a holograph that shows me the state of your organs, brain, spinal cord and nervous system. It then sends that information to a database where we can compare and review your results. It's incredibly thorough and about ninety percent accurate. We can use it to pick up virus, bacteria, disease, blockages and compromised organs, and it can work through your DNA and chromosomes.

Everything in the universe has its own frequency and vibration - that's how we see colours differently, how water is liquid and how a boot is hard. This practice uses those frequencies in your body as a messenger.

From then on, everybody's different. So that's when I use nutrition, homeopathy, vibration remedies and herbal medicine - anything that'll help the individual I'm working with. I like to use many different fields because it's important to understand each individual to treat them properly, rather than using a blanket cover. We work through body, mind and spirit.

Are there any standout hardships you've come across?

It can be really emotionally exhausting; I'm a sensitive person and I take a lot on personally. I'd take cases home and stay up all night, constantly trying to work on them to find the answers. The cases I take are quite difficult ones where blood and stool tests haven't worked, so it can be quite a challenge. The longer you practise though, the better you become at separating work from home.

Can you tell me about The Secret Kitchen's cookbook and the vision behind this project?

The book started as an art passion project because photography has been a hobby for years. It has folk remedies and recipes for each season that are largely plant-based and gluten-free and it's a combination of naturopathy and plant-based eating, as well as a bit of metaphysics with the moon cycles. It includes lifestyle practices such as the right time to clean out the cupboards or spend time with friends, or why to detoxify in spring and how seasons can affect our moods. I call it intuitive eating because it's how our body is supposed to eat, through seasonal, moon and yin and yang cycles.

I hope to help people become in tune with their own senses, rather than follow diets, because I saw a lot of pressure and problems with eating disorders and diets through my work. In my book, I use senses like how certain food makes you feel, your relationship with it and how to create self-love through what we eat, rather than self-sabotage. The whole book has been made with the environment in mind. It's self-published on recycled paper and printed locally with plant inks.

Do no harm. It's simple, but it can be applied in a lot of ways. It can shake the world.

What, in your words, is the importance of community?

Supporting local and within your community can have a really big impact in many different ways. Local businesses and startups are the little people who generally have certain ingrained values. They've started something from love and passion, which can often be felt.

Gluten is a really good example of why you should shop local. People ask me all the time why gluten is bad for our bodies, but actually, it's not. It's how it's grown and how we consume it that's the problem. Most of the world's gluten is grown from genetically

modified seed from big agricultural companies to make it grow faster and bigger so there's more profit. The problem lies with this seed and the manufacturing of these crops. If we were to eat bread from our neighbour, locally from their own crop and mill, made properly and eaten fresh, it'll have no preservatives and you likely won't react to it because the gluten and wheat are actually normal.

It's the same with industries such as dairy. If we're consuming fresh, organic, unpasteurised, unhomogenised milk from a happy cow, we don't have the skin or gut problems that we see so often from people eating dairy. What's normal of the industry is mass production, antibiotics, pesticides, artificial insemination and stress hormones in the milk, then it's pasteurised and homogenised, then filled with sugars and preservatives so it can sit on a shelf.

If we start to become aware of mass production and the importance placed on profitability over real food, as well as start supporting our communities who are putting care, love, positive energy and good intention into products, we have the ability to shift the world hugely. This is why community is so important.

What, to you, is the importance of supporting nature's rhythms?

If you look at the Shamans in India, they still practise things like telepathy and spirituality because they've continued to develop it for many centuries and have hugely heightened senses because of it. But most of us live within concrete - in front of computer and television screens and with our cellphones - which interrupts our frequencies, so over years we have lost this ability and intuitiveness.

When we go out into nature, on bush walks or into the ocean, we feel much better. That's because of the metaphysics and vibrational energies nature emits. We, as humans, respond to this and it heightens our senses.

Eating seasonally is a very simple way of coming back to that intuitive nature and working with those frequencies. If we follow the seasons, we can also see that certain foods grow in certain seasons because they have specific nutritional elements that our bodies require for that time.

What does a better world mean to you?

For me, it means everything working in perfect

...this life has been ingrained in me. I grew up during communism and didn't have a lot of money, so we lived off our gardens because we had to.

unity - animal, plants, people, the environment. A natural flow of energy and life restored.

Do you live by any mantra?

Do no harm. It's simple, but it can be applied in a lot of ways. It can shake the world.

Do you meditate?

Going for a swim or surf in the morning or spending time in my kitchen is my meditation and I try to do these things whenever possible.

What does success mean to you?

I think it's about inner peace. It's not about what we have externally but finding that internal balance. Things like work, lifestyle and relationships can all equate externally to our internal balance and happiness. But this can be hard to achieve in 2020 and beyond, we have bills to pay and commitments that we can't ignore. We're so busy, it's hard to balance everything and only allow time for those things that feed our soul and create that peace.

In the world of environmental sustainability, what's an innovative company you'd recommend?

The Hemp Temple in Byron Bay is one that comes to mind. There are so many, but I really love what they're doing for sustainable fashion and the change they're creating through the awareness within their marketing. They also do really great things for equality within men and women, young and old, no matter your shape or size. They're celebrating the human form, which is beautiful.

Where do you hope to be five years from now?

In a perfect world, growing a family with a big garden and lots of herbs. And not having to hustle for money, just being able to slow down and live well.

If we start to become aware of mass production and the importance placed on profitability over real food, we have the ability to shift the world hugely.

AOTEA MADE
THERAPEUTIC GOODS

TAMA TOKI

GREAT BARRIER ISLAND

How did your upbringing contribute to Aotea Made?

I grew up on Great Barrier Island which was largely my inspiration for the company. My childhood was spent in a Māori community in the north of the island - life's a bit different there, being so removed from civilisation. You live with nature and grow up amongst the bush.

> We'd go down and rise with the sun each day - you become intrinsically connected to nature that way.

Many people have no power, and if they do it's a private generator. Back then, our house was really just a little cabin with a toilet outside. We'd do things like collect our water from the stream, and you'd have to drive about half an hour until you get cell service. We'd go down and rise with the sun each day - you become intrinsically connected to nature that way. My grandmother raised me through much of my adolescence, while my mother worked in town, and we became really close. She taught me a lot about how the bush worked and the principles and practices of tikanga. I intuitively learnt a lot about herbal practices and the circadian rhythm. It was a pretty unique upbringing that you don't really get these days.

It was this upbringing and understanding that led me to starting Aotea in the hopes of utilising our native herbs and remedies in a way that gives back to the island.

What did you set out to achieve?

At age twelve I left the island and went to Auckland Grammar School. I felt a sense of responsibility, coming from a small community, to give back to my home. I went on to study law but still felt at my core this real desire to find a way to give back. I wanted to make a faster and more direct impact on the island. Now for us at Aotea Made, we gift scholarship grants to provide financial support for Māori youth within our community so they can participate in a high level of schooling off of the island, as there are no high schools on the island. We also work to support Great Barrier's ecosystem and provide job opportunities for locals.

It was the herbs that inspired the products, but it was the mandate of giving back to that community that inspired the business as a whole. We're currently working on lots of exciting developments to invest more into Great Barrier's future.

How has the company grown?

We started with our herbalist tonic drink range in 2015 at the farmers' markets in Parnell, Auckland, and we now have more than 250 stockists globally. We scaled up quite quickly, distributing to cafés and boutique supermarkets before moving on to larger chain supermarkets nationwide.

We brought out our Mānuka honey in 2017, initially using our own hives but now working with an apiary on the island. Our topical products were launched in 2018 to further diversify the company. We're starting to work on planting out more Kawakawa, Mānuka and Kūmeraho on the island now so that we can make our own oils and distillations within our distillery which has recently been built there.

What have been some key learning experiences?

I think being really adaptable in business is key. You need to look at the business objectively to make decisions, rather than acting emotionally and having a slow death, so to speak. For us this has recently come in the form of dropping our tonics range so we can focus more on our topical skincare and Mānuka products. With the tonic being a lower price point item, we found the workload and ingredients going into the product didn't leave a healthy profit margin to justify its continuation, so we feel investing time and energy into other products is a better fit. For me personally it was also about staying true and authentic to our Māori identity and remedies, so things like distributing the tonic on an international scale didn't sit right. I began to feel as though it was pulling too far from its roots, both physically and

WILD KINSHIP — CONVERSATIONS WITH CONSCIOUS ENTREPRENEURS

spiritually, and I didn't want the educational side of the product to be lost. It's really about recognising these trends before they sink you - we try to be really nimble and pivot before there's an issue.

Another key lesson I've learnt is that you can be the smartest and most diligent and conscientious guy, but if you're in the wrong industry or jumping in at the wrong time, you're going to be going up against a brick wall. Similarly, if you're in an industry with tail winds or favourable growth prospects, once your core foundation is set you can let the rising tide lift the boat.

How would you best explain tikanga Māori?

Simply put, it means that we (in Māori culture) believe in true sustainability and as tangata whenua, we are kaitiaki [guardians] of the natural world and its resources. These practices and philosophies are taken into account in everything we do at Aotea Made. For example, we ensure we leave enough honey in the hives for the bees over winter.

I intuitively learnt a lot about herbal practices and the circadian rhythm.

Can you tell us more about the Māori cultural aspects that set Aotea Made apart?

Making sure we're always aligning our practices with basic principles of a tikanga framework and ensuring it's implemented across all parts of the business is a core value that likely sets us apart. For example, we only pick from the north-facing side of the plant because it gets the most light, and we learn to recognise which plants are more hardy, meaning we can take a lot more from them. We're aware of these things in both growing and harvesting our products.

We've more recently taken on some pretty heavy research with laboratories who are isolating plant agents in the flora we're working with to better understand their medicinal properties too, which is really exciting.

Science seems to really be acknowledging and giving credibility to the methods of holistic and spiritual practices in recent years, which is interesting.

What, in your words, is the importance of community?

Community is super important. I've grown up largely with whānau and community at the forefront because of my Māori culture. As humans, we're tribal beings, so having that place of belonging and support systems within our community is integral to our existence. But I've actually more recently become interested in this global shift towards identity politics and narratives where individualism is just as important. There's huge benefits to the sovereignty of an individual. I think it's important to figure out who you are as a person alone and not to fall into stereotypes of who you're supposed to be. It can be a fine but important balance to have that commitment to community, while also fostering your own sense of individuality.

Similarly, if you're in an industry with tail winds or favourable growth prospects, once your core foundation is set you can let the rising tide lift the boat.

What's the importance of supporting nature's rhythms?

I think it's about being mindful and respecting the ecosystem you're working within. The spirits within nature are far more intricate than what we see or intellectualise. Within Aotea, we're careful to propagate only from species we already have on the island or from our own nursery. We're not bringing anything new from elsewhere in New Zealand or the world. We look into how the flora works within itself and we don't disturb these intricacies; instead we work to aid them.

What does a better world mean to you?

I'm really interested in the postmodernist/modernist debate and think it's a theory that will go on forever. I'm not sure of the answer but I think human nature can still be a pretty horrible thing, despite us thinking that we're superior. But if humans could fully understand and live with the consciousness

that happiness, success and wellness is less about your external environment and more about what comes cognitively from within, we could create a better world. If we could truly live with that as an anchor, this would allow us to deal with the tragedy of life and become better people.

What's the company's biggest success?

The most fulfilling part of what we do is giving back to the community.

What would be your biggest sacrifice in running Aotea Made?

I'm not sure I'd call it a sacrifice - a sacrifice to me is something that you've given up that leads to resentment. I guess financial freedom has been a challenging one, but I would by no means call it a sacrifice because I love what we're doing so much. I guess there are other entrepreneurial pursuits that I would love to do, but there's not enough hours in the day. I'll work out a way to do them anyway though.

Science seems to really be acknowledging and giving credibility to the methods of holistic and spiritual practices in recent years.

What are your biggest passions beyond Aotea Made?

I'm really interested in the world's future and what it will look like.

We're doing a lot of work and research surrounding renewable energy possibilities within Aotea Made. The Barrier itself is creating a sort of echo chamber of possibilities around renewable energies, because the general infrastructure is already established we want to launch a hybrid energy system. Anything innovation-related is really interesting and something I'm super passionate about.

Do you have any daily rituals?

I learnt transcendental meditation in Northern India years ago and do that every morning. Otherwise I find reading or going for a run or surf is really good for me.

What does success mean to you?

Personal growth in whatever field you're naturally attracted to at that time. The feeling of growing in an emotional or physical sense is important. I think reaching goals and targets you set for yourself is personal success.

In the world of environmental sustainability, what's an innovative company you'd recommend?

Elon Musk from Tesla is obviously incredible, but I guess sometimes you need to question the motivation of those huge companies and wonder if they're really creating positive change across the board. Empresa de Electricidade da Madeira is a small company that's teamed up with Renault in Europe to create a smart electric ecosystem on a few islands off Portugal, which is super cool.

If humans could fully understand and live with the consciousness that happiness, success and wellness is less about your external environment and more about what comes cognitively from within, we could create a better world.

Where do you hope to be five years from now?

Continuing to make inroads toward helping people on the island. I hope we have some more positive infrastructure in place by then that really improves the quality of life and aids the island holistically.

There's huge benefits to the sovereignty of an individual. I think it's important to figure out who you are as a person alone and not to fall into stereotypes of who you're supposed to be.

HAKEA
SWIMWEAR

CASEY EASTWELL

NEW BRIGHTON

How did Hakea come to be?

I always knew I wanted to work for myself but didn't want to do something just for the hell of it. I was previously working in Melbourne as a graphic designer for a clothing label and was often going away on surf trips overseas. For a while I was on the hunt for a really good rash guard because I didn't feel super comfortable surfing in a bikini, and I really struggled to find something that felt like good quality and was my style. Bathers were getting smaller and smaller, and offering less coverage. As soon as I realised there was a gap in the market, Hakea was born. I quit my job and moved to Bali to start working on it. I now work with two factories over there and they're really amazing. I do the designs here in Byron, then go over to check samples before we launch any new styles.

What did you set out to achieve?

I wanted to create a rash guard that was both functional and flattering and in turn promote and support body confidence. I wanted women to feel beautiful and comfortable being in their swimwear down the beach. I wanted it to be practical and thoughtful, as well as really versatile. Being able to go from beach to town by throwing on a pair of shorts to create an outfit really appealed to me. I wanted the brand to be sustainable, not just in the fabrics and packaging or the longevity of the product but by having pieces you can mix and match or wear as clothing items, too.

It was important to me that it wasn't a fast fashion label, so I was really conscious of how I could build this brand in a way that fit into that ethos, which is why Hakea is quite small. We do small production runs that are topped up as required and don't bring out a new range every season. Hakea pieces are designed to last forever - they're simple and classic.

What have been some key learning experiences?

I found there's a lot of isolation when you're running a business yourself, which can get pretty real. I'm lucky a lot of my friends around Byron also work for themselves.

Starting the business was actually easier than I thought, I had good contacts for production lines from my previous job so once I found the courage and solidified the range, I had so much momentum. Nurturing and growing a business is much harder, you can become quite stretched, being a solo operation, but I'm learning to outsource which has been really helpful.

What, in your words, is the importance of community?

Byron, like Bali, is a really supportive community that nurtures a lot of startups and freelance creatives. They're both about living that good, free, relaxed lifestyle out in the elements, which suited the brand and our offering (being stylish and sun protective swimwear). Starting a company in the right location that fits your ethos is really important for its success, but also for your own creative output and sense of belonging.

What's the difference between your products and regular swimwear on the market?

I try to design pieces that are purposeful and versatile and then test them on a bunch of different bodies. All of our swimsuits are UPF 50+ in a range of earthy colours. We've started using a recycled fabric for more of our styles that is made up of ECONYL, a regenerated nylon fibre made from ocean waste and fabric mills and Xtra-life Lycra which adds to the longevity of the product.

I've visited both of the factories I work with a number of times and have a great relationship with them. One is super small and is run by two girls who are a similar age to me – it's just a bunch of friends who left their old factory jobs. The other factory is run by an Australian woman and she does a really good job at keeping the work and pay standards really fair.

Where can we find your products?

We have a few stockists in the US, but mostly through my online store and Australian retailers.

What does a better world mean to you?

People being more conscious. More conscious in how they treat themselves and one another, as well as the world around them. We all get so busy and forget to slow down and recognise the truly important things.

What, to you, is the company's biggest success?

Just to hear that other women are resonating with Hakea or seeing a woman's face light up when she tries on a Hakea piece for the first time.

What would be your biggest sacrifice in running Hakea?

Probably my free time and freedom in general. That luxury of being able to be selfish with your time and money, instead of constantly investing it back into the company. For the most part, I'm so happy to do that because watching my brand grow is a great feeling, but it's often at the sacrifice of yourself. This experience has taught me that you can live well with less though.

What's your go-to when you're in a creative rut?

I go straight down to the beach, or out for a wine with friends.

Who's your biggest inspiration?

I look up to the American designer Jesse Kamm. Her business model and ethos is really inspiring and so beautiful.

Do you live by any mantra?

"The mere fact of being able to call your job your passion is success in my eyes." – Alicia Vikander.

In the world of environmental sustainability, what's an innovative company you'd recommend?

Aquafil the company behind ECONYL. Their circular model is something we can all learn from. The planet's resources are finite so we need to come up wtih solutions to recycle, recreate or remould what we already have.

Where do you hope to be five years from now?

Still loving what I am doing and being able to use Hakea as a louder platform to promote a simpler kind of lifestyle.

This experience has taught me that you can live well with less.

CASEY EASTWELL — HAKEA

We all get so busy and forget to slow down and recognise the truly important things.

NATURE BABY
CHILDRENSWEAR

JACOB + GEORGIA FAULL

AUCKLAND

How did Nature Baby come to be and how has it grown?

Georgia: It started with the birth of our first child, now twenty years ago. Because there weren't any baby clothes made from natural fabrics (definitely no organics), it was all polar fleece and synthetics, it really was about what we wanted for our own family. We started out in the front room of our Ponsonby flat as a mail order company for the first nine months. We opened our first store in 1999 in Grey Lynn, just across the road from our current flagship store, so we've been within this community for a really long time and it's a special place to us.

Jacob: We now have three stores across Auckland, along with a big online presence, but we never strayed too far or grew too fast that it took away from life at home with a young and growing family. We could've done a lot more over the years, but it didn't fit with our family values and priorities. It's meant we've been able to focus heavily on our core values and who we are. Business is greedy by nature and it always plays into this idea of profit, which is necessary of course, but if that growth extends past you, it can pull you in the wrong direction.

> ## Business is greedy by nature and it always plays into this idea of profit, which is necessary of course, but if that growth extends past you, it can pull you in the wrong direction.

Are there any standout hardships you've come across?

Jacob: I think a lot of hardships come back to having financial balance - that can be the biggest stress from day one, starting up, but then having that longevity and continuing to grow comfortably. This is something you have to be able to manage financially and physiologically right throughout the process.

Georgia: I find the hardest thing is being a jack-of-all-trades, from HR to design to finance, you just have to be everywhere at once which can be exhausting at times.

What have been some key learning experiences?

Jacob: Keeping things basic. Knowing the bones of your product or business plan and being careful not to diversify too much. Making sure you have that foundation solid and expanding from there. There can be a lot of temptations when you're working in so many different areas across the business, you can get pulled in different directions that lead you off the path. At one point, we were going up to seven years old but there's really enough within baby to grow and get right without branching out into different avenues.

In hindsight, a business degree would've been handy. Learning on the street is good, but a few papers, especially now we're forty staff in, would've been helpful. I'd also say finding a business mentor early on is a good move.

The age of Nature Baby is incredible, can you explain how you've evolved over time?

Georgia: The industry has changed of course - back then there were really only places like The Baby Factory. It was all bright and synthetic with teddy bears everywhere. Nature Baby specifically hasn't actually changed in style that much, it's simply become more refined over the years. There's been a huge shift within the organics industry though, it's much more accepted and understood now which has helped us portray our message more clearly.

Jacob: It's really only been in the last five years that people are starting to understand the importance of organic cotton and what we wear (as opposed to what we ingest) and really care about the production line.

How do you find work life balance as a family-run company?

Georgia: Jacob and I have quite opposite natures,

but that means we work quite well together in business. It ends up nicely balanced in regard to our strengths and weaknesses. We both have the same goals and ethics for the brand, so we're moving in the same direction. I work with the factories and on the garment design and fabric sourcing. We were so young when we got into it, I didn't have any experience in fashion, but I guess I always enjoyed learning from an art and design perspective.

Jacob: When we're not working, we'll gravitate towards the same things. We both did arts degrees involving art history and we really like concepts around growth and things like new neighbourhoods and developments. But then when we work together, we're quite different. In any working relationship, it's about understanding that conflict and tension are positive and finding a way to work through it. I work within branding operations, financial planning, warehousing and shop leases, which I enjoy, although I find myself missing the creative side a little bit.

What's the difference between your production line and that of regular clothing on the market?

Georgia: Our garments are made in India - we have two amazing factories, one that we've worked with for the last seventeen years and they manufacture about eighty percent of what we do. It's really nice to have that close relationship with them. We've done lots of origin trips over the years, right back to meeting the growers in rural areas. We're the same age as the couple who owns the factory and we've both really grown together over the years.

> It's only more recently that people are understanding the environmental impact of their choices. We can't see the devastated cotton fields here or the families and farmers who've been taken advantage of by big agriculture companies.

Jacob: They're located in the state where Gandhi comes from, where the revolution of making their own cloth was founded. India itself is a pretty crazy chaotic country, it's half beautiful, spiritual life and colour and half death and caste system - both in the view all the time. It becomes this real dichotomy over acceptance of how things are along with potential to be really connected with what you're doing. I think it's that part that makes these people so good at what they do and have incredible attention to detail. They want to make sure the cotton is of the highest quality, and that everything is made in the best way. For us, this means the clothes just last and last. We had the highest resale of baby clothes on Trade Me last year, and there's entire Facebook buy and sell pages just for Nature Baby, where clothes are going around and around and lasting through four or five families with multiple kids.

How does that sort of thing sit with you from a business perspective, seeing the resale of your products?

Georgia: We love seeing that. We want to find a way to support it because it's a really positive thing. We'd rather sell less per capita with higher quality and longevity of our products - being able to reuse our products and reduce that consumption is super important. We never started Nature Baby with profit at the forefront. Having enough of an income so that we can grow and offer more to the supply chain and customer is our target.

And that's actually the beauty with small business and startups, you have the option and potential to work over these emerging platforms, whereas already established, bigger companies become so ossified and set in their ways that they don't want to change - because they feel they have nothing to change to.

Can you talk us through the importance of ethical manufacturing and what effect this has on the environment and human welfare?

Jacob: Our factories only use organic cotton, whereas other factories use both - so our guys are really focused and committed to the cause. They have great relationships with not only the growers but also the government for green initiatives - the husband sits on a panel for the UN and talks about bringing sustainable practices into one of the biggest markets in the world. They really care about the whole picture, from ensuring local

Indian families have someone at home cooking for their family and making a living, to also shaking things up on a much larger scale internationally.

It's only more recently that people are understanding the environmental impact of their choices. We can't see the devastated cotton fields here or the families and farmers who've been taken advantage of by big agriculture companies. We're so removed from the farmers who are drinking the poison and killing themselves because they're drowning in debt, their land won't produce anymore because of years of pesticides and fertilisers, or they've had their farms taken away from them due to financial strain. But that's the norm.

Why are organics so important?

Georgia: I think it goes beyond the product itself - it's the entire production process. If something is certified organic that covers things like labour and social responsibility as well, so it's your own health, the health of the planet and the health of the people who are making the product.

Jacob: Right, so not only are you going to be healthy but you're going to have a planet you can actually live on that's going to be healthy. The negative effects can seem subtle; the way we use chemicals and toxins now is such a usual part of life, but the buildup of these synthetics becomes so accumulative, you don't really start to notice until it's too late. On one trip to India we asked the factory workers what some of the differences were between working with organic cotton every day, rather than inorganic, and they said, *"We don't have respiratory problems anymore"*. That's a huge outcome. And then on a totally different scale, in New Zealand a few years back there was a popular children's clothing company which tested positive for formaldehyde in its fabrics. Not only can that go into your skin, your largest organ but when it goes through the wash, that waste is going out into our waterways and oceans in which we swim. The damaging ripple effects are huge.

How do your production methods help aid environmental sustainability?

Sustainability is at the forefront of all we do - from our store build, to the buttons on the clothing, to the wool in the mattress, to the composting of our vegetable starch bags. But we're constantly adjusting and thinking of new ways to be better. We've recently started using refillable pencils

instead of pens, for example. There are so many little things you don't think about until you start digging.

What does a better world mean to you?

Georgia: I would say a circular world. One that's more sustainable and isn't using more resources than we need.

Jacob: Connectivity and consciousness. If you know who you are, who's in your community and the effect your choices have, then you'll be more aware to make better choices. Organic is just a by-product of being conscious. It's easy to feel disempowered in the world because you're just one person, but in reality, there's so much one person can do - especially when we band together as a community. The whole world is actually built on the theory that one person can change things - look at religion for an example of that; Buddha, Jesus, even Steve Jobs. But seriously, whatever you're doing, you can make a difference and increase your own quality of life, too.

> The negative effects can seem subtle; the way we use chemicals and toxins now is such a usual part of life, you don't really start to notice until it's too late.

What, in your words, is the importance of community?

Jacob: I think it comes back to that connectivity and supporting one another, especially in small business. We feel quite passionate about nurturing small communities like Grey Lynn to be more liveable, with things like bike lanes and plenty of parking, so we're more connected and supportive of one another. Knowing your local butcher and who bakes your bread has a lot of value for you personally and for those business' livelihoods. So, being someone who leads by example within your own business ethics and products, but also by supporting others (whether that's shopping with them, or in our case sometimes in a business mentor capacity) helps to nurture your community.

What, in your eyes, is the company's biggest success?

Georgia: I think there have been some pretty cool moments where we've been in J.Crew on Madison Avenue in New York, or people like Halle Berry have reached out to us and love our products. And those things might sound like consumerism, but really, they're just examples of how far our message has gone and it being positively received - which is a form of energy and important to take stock of. You put a lot of energy out there and those moments help you realise the scale of what you've created. They help you get that energy back.

Jacob: For me, it's being able to create an entirely organic store - from the clothes (obviously) to the furniture, the mattresses and the toys. And within the fit-out, using sustainable timbers and artisan light shades. Every little detail has been taken into consideration. I love the idea of creating these spaces all over the world, where local artists, designers and curators can be found in one place, bringing together that community wherever you are - be it Grey Lynn, Sydney or London.

How does environmental sustainability spill into your personal life?

Georgia: It does across the board. But that was why we started Nature Baby - because we've always eaten organic, composted, recycled and used cloth nappies. It was when we came across an industry that didn't have any options that the business was born, so it's quite ingrained in our lifestyle. There are little things that we still want to improve though - I'd really love to trade my car in for an electric one.

Jacob: We're not perfect of course, but when you start paying attention to your own lifestyle you start to notice more and more that can be done. Recently we've been trying to remove plastic from our lives, which has actually been a little difficult. Not so much in obvious things like shopping bags, but more so being aware of not buying foods that are packaged in plastic and thinking of alternatives for picking up dog poo or lining the rubbish bin.

What are your biggest passions beyond Nature Baby?

Jacob: I think if I wasn't doing this I'd be running an art gallery. I like the idea of working with artists and curating different ideas and spaces.

Who's your biggest inspiration?

Georgia: For me, it's women who've risen to the top of their field. Someone like Vandana Shiva, who's an Indian ecologist, or Anita Roddick who started The Body Shop.

Jacob: I'd say artists in history who've grown through great change; people like William Morris at the beginning of industrialisation in England, and how he looked to create an industry and community around making things. It's that mix of artist and a commercial practice that gets me. But also, people like Damien Hirst, Sarah Lucas and Rachel Whiteread in the art world who, at a pivotal time in my life, changed the way I understood or looked at things beyond my consciousness.

What does success mean to you?

Georgia: Health and happiness, and to be honest, financial security is unfortunately an important aspect of that - it gives you the freedom to live well.

In the world of environmental sustainability, what's an innovative company you'd recommend and why?

Jacob: For me, it's probably Kōkako. The precision and depth within the company's ethics is incredible and they're telling a really important story. I feel like I've learnt a lot from Mike.

Georgia: Ecostore is really inspiring – I've looked to them a lot, especially when we started out.

Where do you hope to be five years from now?

Jacob: I'd love to be in Portland with a pop-up shop and gallery (I'm not sure how or where that fits in), but also travelling and continuing what we've started here.

Georgia: We do have really big dreams for Nature Baby's future, it's just about how we're going to get from here to there and facilitate them that's the unknown.

> ...whatever you're doing, you can make a difference and increase your own quality of life, too.

Organic is just a
by-product of being
conscious. It's easy
to feel disempowered
in the world because
you're just one person,
but in reality, there's
so much one person
can do - especially
when we band together
as a community.

ANDREW MORRIS
+ AMANDA CALLAN

BILLINUDGEL

How did Church Farm General Store come to be?

Amanda: It all happened very much by accident, we were just doing something we loved to do and people responded really positively to the products we were making. Everything evolved from the church building itself and things fell into place; we were really excited about having all of this land to utilise so we started planting out chillis and herbs and found we had an abundance. To try and use them up, Andrew starting smoking chillis and making sauces. I was studying naturopathy so started drying herbs to put into soaps for our personal use.

Andrew had previously built the little roadside stall for our excess fruit and vegetables from the garden. We put the soaps and sauces out there too and started getting these cute notes in the money box from people saying how much they loved the products. We'd even get messages like *"I've got a shop on the Gold Coast and would love to stock your products,"* which we thought was really weird. Did a real shop really want our little things? We were just mucking around!

Looking back, it was the good life. We had a little baby and we were just cruising round pickling stuff and making soap all day, we weren't worried about where it was going or what we were doing with our lives.

How did you come across the church building?

Andrew: We were previously living in Brisbane and Sydney where I'd been slogging it out for years working in the music industry, so when we moved into the area it felt like a nice opportunity to do something different. We suddenly had all this time.

We'd just started looking to buy, and were driving with Amanda's parents through the countryside one day when Amanda's dad, as a joke, turned left and drove into the driveway of the church and said, *"Imagine if this was for sale?"* We all laughed, but then lo and behold it had a little 'for sale' sign up. We called the number straight away and negotiated directly with the Catholic Church to purchase the house.

Amanda: Over time, we lifted the church up and renovated the interior floor plan, planted hundreds of native trees and some vegetable gardens, and got some chooks. Instead of a housewarming party we had a tree raising party where everyone brought a native plant instead, so that they all had a sense of connection to the land here and the forest planted around us. We salvaged a lot of stuff during the renovations and used heaps of recycled materials or secondhand products for the house and gardens. It's largely repurposed and recycled, which we really like. We don't often buy new things; I love to hunt out second hand finds and restore furniture instead.

> We don't have everything mapped out with targets we want to hit or anything, we still want our lifestyle to come first.

How has the company grown?

Amanda: We officially established ourselves in 2013. We grew and made everything here at home in the beginning - there were crates and jars everywhere! We'd be trying to cook and eat dinner while shuffling huge crate pots of sauces around. We'd put the kids to bed and sit up late labelling everything.

Andrew: We built the little black shed in the yard originally to make soaps from, then we started using it as storage for orders. It's about two by three metres and now we have a 200 square metre factory. Once we finally got the warehouse, it all went a bit crazy and took off. We've never had a loan for the business because it grew with us in stages over time. We never went and sought out stockists either, they've come to us through the likes of social media which is great because we don't really like to hustle in regard to the sales side of things.

Amanda: We don't have everything mapped out with targets we want to hit or anything, we still want our lifestyle to come first.

Andrew: If it's blowing offshore and we've dropped the kids at school we still want to be able to get into it. We'd both love the business to succeed of course, and we're stoked with how it's gone so far, but I don't think we want to be the next Richard Branson or anything. As long as we can provide for our family, employ good local people and enjoy what we are doing, that's really all we want.

What have been some key learning experiences?

Amanda: We're always learning stuff. Because we have more creative backgrounds, we've been learning the business side of things day-to-day. We've worked with a local not-for-profit company called Sourdough that basically helps small businesses within the area by assigning mentors. It's cool to have someone offering advice like that. Cashflow is always a tough one for any small business too, so learning to navigate that has been a big learning curve.

I think the importance of good staff is also really underrated. Having the right personalities in the mix is crucial; we spend a lot of time together, so you don't want it to be weird vibes. We're really lucky with the little crew we've got.

Where can we find your products?

Andrew: We do four markets locally and two in Sydney, plus you'll find our products on our website and through wholesale - which would be the biggest platform. We have national distributors which take that side of things off our hands, but we stock roughly 215 stores worldwide. It's quite funny sometimes, we'll just go into a shop and be like *oh look they have our stuff*. We make around 3000 soaps and bottle around 1000 condiments a week, and we do other jobs like 'ghost soaping' where we make product for The Source.

How does the production process differ from that of standard condiments and soaps on the market?

Amanda: Everything's handmade in small batches, made with local or our own produce. It's quite labour intensive, hands-on cooking at the warehouse. We really like using ingredients there's an abundance of, too; making sure there's no waste, or even in some cases using waste products from other local companies. For example, we collaborated with the restaurant Three Blue Ducks from The Farm and made a ground coffee bar, as well as Stone & Wood, a local brewery, and made a beer-infused bar.

Our soaps are made through cold processed methods - there's no fake anything, or things like palm oil. It's a soft, nurturing way to make a soap, which is then really soft on your skin, too. We use ingredients like local hemp and macadamia oil and infuse herbs into them.

Andrew: We have a really simple inline production in the factory, it's pretty lo-fi. There are also no numbers, emulsifiers or creepy things on the labels in the food or sauces; it's just made traditionally with real ingredients. It's a bit of a weird combo, the sauces and soaps. At the time, it was just good versions of things we wanted in our lives and couldn't find!

How do you find the work life balance with a young family?

Amanda: We have two boys; Banjo is six and Percy is three. Having two kids in Byron is like having no kids, all of our friends have like five each. Andrew is kind of an at-home-mum through the week with the boys' school runs and evening activities. I started studying naturopathy in 2010, so I'm up in the city studying through the week.

Andrew: I drop the boys off to school and daycare, check the surf and then head into work. It's a pretty good balance.

What are your biggest passions beyond this?

Amanda: Probably still what we were doing before this; for me naturopathy and herbalism. I really enjoy the one-on-one nature of working with people and being able to help them. Andrew was working full time as a guitarist, touring with a friend. So, music and surfing.

Andrew: ...and cricket.

Do you live by any mantra?

Andrew: Amanda's is *"How good is life?!"* (ha-ha)

Amanda: Yeah, I'm always saying that, after an epic surf where there's double rainbows and dolphins and you feel like you're in this different dimension. Or if we've had a real good day at the beach with our friends. Lately we've been having a glass of red on the beach after dinner then going back out for a surf - moments like that I'm always like *"how good is this?"* I get really pumped when there's a big group of us down the beach, the kids are all playing, the dads are manning the BBQ and all the mums are out surfing, and then we'll swap over.

Who are your biggest inspirations?

Amanda: Mine are these super old naturopath women that no one knows, who live with their goats in European countries. I've become sort of obsessed with them.

Do you have any daily rituals?

Andrew: We have a cooked breakfast together every morning. We prioritise food in this house quite a lot. Things like that, a cuppa, and keeping an eye on the surf.

Amanda: Andrew makes me a cup of tea every morning. Unless he's grumpy with me - I'll always know if I don't get a tea in the morning.

In the world of environmental sustainability, what's an innovative company you'd recommend?

Amanda: Seed & Sprout are pretty awesome, and Arnhem does some cool stuff within fashion – they're really legit and doing so much for that industry that's come at their own cost. The farmers around here are really cool too, it's hard work but their output is so good for the whole community.

Where do you hope to be five years from now?

Amanda: I want to die in this church, I love it here. I would love to open a clinic and dispensary with a bunch of friends in town once I've finally finished studying though.

Andrew: Yeah, just where we are, raising our boys, watching them grow and living a good life.

WĀ COLLECTIVE
MENSTRUAL CUPS

OLIE BODY

WELLINGTON

How did your past contribute to Wā Collective?

I was midway through my studies in chemistry and religion and was feeling a little lost. One key thing I'd taken from these two polar opposite fields was a deep interest in how the world works. I decided to move to India and just before I was due to leave, I attended a seminar held by an organisation called Days for Girls. They sew reusable cloth pad kits and during their talk they said, *"If a girl gets her period and she has a lack of resources, she drops out of school"* – which means the cycle of poverty continues. This really struck a chord with me, so I arrived in India with this huge bag of menstrual cloth kits to give out.

I ended up living in the rural foothills of the Himalayas in a wee village for eight months, and I made good friends with the local nurse there. One day she asked me to water the plants, even though it was usually a morning ritual for her. When I asked why, she said, *"Because I'm dirty, I'm bleeding. If I water the plants now, they'll die."* That was a huge turning point for me, and I realised that there was a lot more to the distribution of the kits than I'd thought.

The nurse and I worked with the young girls in the community, each sharing our knowledge and talking about periods openly and with respect. These girls had tears in their eyes when they received their kits – this was life-changing for many of them. We set about creating a supply chain in India to get the materials so these women could sew the kits themselves, which was actually a lot more powerful.

How did Wā Collective come to be?

Returning home, I felt inspired and called to continue my education, as I had access to it, when many others don't. At university one day, I was staring at a bowl of free condoms and started to wonder why there was a bowl of condoms but not menstrual products. I researched to find one in every three students had skipped class before because they didn't have access to menstrual products. For me, that really brought the issue of period poverty home. It was as much a community issue as it was a global one.

I started reaching out to pad and tampon companies but learnt that New Zealand alone sends 357 million disposable menstrual products to landfill each year, so these single-use items are harming not only us but the planet, too. I eventually started researching menstrual cups as they seemed to tick all the boxes. I bought a cup and was super excited about using it, but when the time came around it didn't work. It hurt, it leaked, it sucked. I was gutted because I thought it could've been a game changer. So, I ended up procuring our own cup – we rolled it out and it grew really quickly from there.

What did you set out to achieve?

A period seems to have become more of a pharmaceutical process than a natural and necessary one. Each month, we're buying into a model promoted through these huge companies because we think we need to. The realisation that I didn't need to be part of the disposable industry was very liberating. We need to educate ourselves and find better options, rather than relying on these toxic ones. Our goal is to help create awareness around these topics while offering a better alternative that benefits your body, your wallet and our planet.

> I didn't want to be setting up a company here that was helping our people, but causing people in other countries to suffer.

How has the company grown?

We officially launched in 2018. In the space of twelve months with our current model, we were able to divert one million disposable sanitary items from landfill (based on the number of cups we'd sold). Collectively, that's also saved our customers $350,000. Imagine the difference that can make long term.

Menstruation can be a taboo topic. Can you talk about Wā Collective's approach to this?

One big issue right from the start was that periods

WILD KINSHIP — CONVERSATIONS WITH CONSCIOUS ENTREPRENEURS

OLIE BODY — WĀ COLLECTIVE

weren't talked about. Because of this, neither gender has been given the tools to talk about periods at all, let alone positively. We're asking for a complete mindset change, behaviour change and change of discourse as much as anything. This taboo has run so deep for so long and has stemmed from a lack of knowledge coupled with the systemic oppression of women, going centuries back. We are still experiencing the hangovers from this here in New Zealand. From a Western perspective, periods still hold ties to shame, embarrassment, confusion and pollution. On the contrary, in some other cultures menstruation is celebrated. Trying to reverse this generational stigma is extremely important and challenging. So, we're speaking about it openly and frankly and with a bit of bloody humor (pun intended), so we can start to shift that dialogue.

Why should we be wary of other menstrual companies and products?

We generally use tampons and pads because this is what we're taught. We're buying into this monthly subscription – and just imagine how much money is getting poured into these companies across the globe. It's huge! And it really doesn't make sense for them to buy into a more sustainable model because the disposable one is so lucrative. The vagina is a hugely sensitive space; tampons are often made from synthetic fabrics filled with harmful toxins that can leach into our bodies. They aren't just absorbing the menstrual blood – they're absorbing all of the natural juices that our bodies need for a healthy pH balance and all of our flora. These products do a massive disservice to our bodies.

How does Wā Collective positively contribute to environmental sustainability?

Each Wā cup offers zero waste and 100 percent traceability through the entire manufacturing process. They're ethically made by our partners in the US, using silicon from Massachusetts. This was really important to me. I didn't want to be setting up a company here that was helping our people but causing people in other countries to suffer. They also last up to ten years, which means you're saving around 2,500 disposables from entering your body and landfill.

We've eliminated all redundant plastic throughout our production chain and all our materials are compostable, recyclable or reusable. We use vegetable dyes and recycled papers, and all of our post is sent in recycled boxes with a note explaining this choice to reiterate our full-cycle approach.

You have a subsidy programme with student associations, can you explain how that works?

Each cup we sell allows us to subsidise a cup for a student in need. We work directly with student associations, which means we engage them in the conversation as well.

What does a better world mean to you?

For me, it's one where we can problem-solve holistically. Where we're making changes that help the planet and the people and take us forward – but not at the expense of the other. Quick solutions that only address the issue at hand but open up ten new problems (either ethically, environmentally or socially) really grate on me. I think we'll have finally grown up when we can look at this world holistically, as a connected space. What's outside is in, and what's inside is out. I think we really need to start recognising that.

What, to you, is the company's biggest success?

There's both the micro and macro. In 2018, we won two sustainable business awards, which was really incredible, especially as we were only eight months in. We were up against huge companies (and their marketing and PR teams), so to take it out and be recognised in that way was phenomenal. But then in a micro sense, it's the emails and messages we get daily from customers, telling us that this little cup has changed their lives.

If money was no object, what would you do differently?

If we could give reusable menstrual products to everyone for free, along with important information, that would be huge. I think we'd see a huge societal shift as people started to understand and connect with their own bodies and awaken that consciousness of the planet.

Do you live by any mantra?

Understanding and truly embodying the notion that there's no such thing as failure. We're a combined product of all our past experiences, and that's what leads us to where we are and who we are now.

Do you have any daily rituals?

I'm really lucky to live by the sea, so every morning

I go and have an ice-cold swim in the ocean. It can be really hard to do some days when it's raining and windy, but it's the best way to start my day.

What does success mean to you?

Livng my authentic self. Allowing myself to do so is really liberating. Society tells us to be someone or something and fit into this certain model or jump through different hoops. I think it's really empowering to just be you instead.

In the world of environmental sustainability, what's an innovative company you'd recommend?

Days for Girls. They lead with such passion and heart and have an incredible global footprint – it really is where it all started for me.

Where do you hope to be five years from now?

I hope that we've solved period poverty in New Zealand, sustainably. This might sound like a big feat, but we really are this tiny country that has so much power to come together as a community and make a massive positive impact together.

I think we'll have finally grown up when we can look at this world holistically, as a connected space. What's outside is in, and what's inside is out.

WILL & BEAR
HATS

LAUREN WILLIAMS + ALEXANDER KNORR

VAN MARTY, ON THE ROAD, AUSTRALIA

How did Will & Bear come to be?

Lauren: We were actually on our very first holiday together in Tasmania about four years ago. The first day we were there, we were on the hunt for a hat for Alex. It was the middle of an Australian summer but all we could find were really daggy options. We ended up fighting over this op shop hat we'd found for the rest of the holiday. During this trip, we started talking about what cool hat brands we knew of and realised there was a real gap in the market. It was actually on that same trip, both of us being really into photography, that we took all these pictures of us exploring – with the op shop hat featuring heavily. It was then we decided to create a hat label that connected the hat and its owner with the outdoors.

How has the company grown?

Lauren: It was a year after that trip that we launched the brand Will & Bear. We didn't have a lot of business experience, so there was a lot of market research and product development to be done. The first year was pretty slow, we were both working our usual day jobs too - I was a mortgage broker and Alex a freelance designer. Now we stock about 120 stores around the world. The wholesale market grew really quickly, and we recently made the call to cap our wholesale accounts. We wanted to slow down and be really selective with who we were stocking, to ensure they fit with our ethos.

Alex: We've tripled our business year on year. This kind of growth can be dangerous in business, but as a startup you kind of have to throw everything in early on and then start refining and slowing down.

Are there any standout hardships you've come across?

Lauren: I think the hardest thing for us personally would be running the company as a couple. There are of course positives as we're both equally invested and passionate about it and really sure of its direction, but we have to be conscious of our down time because we're together all the time and our work can be very 'freelance' – sometimes we just work and work and work. We need to be mindful of setting boundaries around that knowing when to switch off for the day, especially when we're living in Marty, our van.

Another big learning curve was managing cash flow and things like inventory and warehouses. We were naturally really good at the marketing and design side, but because the company grew quickly, it was hard to get a handle on the more finicky side of the business. We ended up getting a business coach in for a year, which was hugely beneficial.

> ...learning to say no is really powerful and important to ensure you're steering your brand in the right direction.

Alex: We found that as you go along you have to accept that there's a level of uncertainty in everything you're doing, and you learn things as they arise. We found that we just had to trust in that and sit back and enjoy the ride. At the time, you're kind of just hanging on for dear life and trying to get through it, but in hindsight, or now with more experience behind us, you learn you can get through anything if you can just take things as they come.

What have been some key learning experiences?

Lauren: At the start, you're so scared the business is going to fail or that you're not doing enough, so you act a lot out of fear and just say yes to everything. But learning to say no is really powerful and important to ensure you're steering your brand in the right direction. Another thing we learnt quite early on is that people really appreciate us being two weird humans who don't know what we're doing. In the beginning, we were really nervous and trying so hard to be professional and serious, but actually dropping that act and being vulnerable makes you more relatable and opens you up to asking for help. That openness within friendships and other businesses was really beneficial. Being able to support one another and bounce ideas around is great.

Alex: I'm sure many business owners can relate to this, but when you've just started out you're a little afraid of sharing ideas and once you finally do, you build this pressure around succeeding. And then you realise that reaching perfection doesn't exist and not what you're actually trying to achieve as a business. I guess leaving yourself open to sharing these battles and learnings helps you grow so much more and pushes you towards being better.

Can you explain the production process of your work?

Lauren: The wool we use is from small farms in Western Australia (WA). The textile industry has a lot of waste - there's loads of off-cuts that we use. Our factory is in Mongolia, which is an old family factory that's been running for seventy-five years. We were stoked to visit it before we launched. They mill the wool there and hand-make the hats. We're excited to be looking into other renewable resources moving forward, too - things like hemp are about to blow up and will be really cool to work with. There are about 101 different hands that go into the production of a hat, so it's a really detailed and in-depth process.

We're all a part of this world so we all need to find a way to positively contribute.

You work with Trees for the Future (trees.org) to aid reforestation, can you talk more about how this partnership works and the impact it has?

Alex: We partnered with Trees for the Future about six months after we launched. It was always the goal, but we wanted to get our feet on the ground first. On the surface it's quite basic - one hat purchased equals ten trees. What the organisation actually does though is really in-depth. Our trees are planted in Senegal, Africa because the land there has been completely depleted from decades of peanut farming. Trees.org finds farmers whose land is ruined and puts them into four-year training programmes so they can learn how to plant food

forests instead. It's an incredible circular programme that helps families and communities from an educational perspective, as well as financially and environmentally. Their harvests also largely contribute to the community's food source by creating an abundance of healthy fruit and vegetables throughout the year. They're also doing amazing work to empower women within the villages. We went to visit them last year for three weeks - it was so amazing to see the effect it's having; you go from a barren dusty desert into this total oasis where there's blooms and bees and birds and all this food. For us as a business, it's an awesome quantifiable measure - we know that to date we've planted more than 400,000 trees through Will & Bear.

What, in your words, is the importance of community?

Lauren: It's everything really, and it's super multi-layered. We actually both had different ideas surrounding community going into it. I wanted it to impact my immediate community, family, friends, staff and our immediate surroundings.

Alex: My idea was more around a global community and how we can affect other people's lives more positively through our business. We're all a part of this world so we all need to find a way to positively contribute. But there's another aspect to community that's become apparent to us too, which is within our own customer base and following. We want to find a way to cultivate this creative community of people - their passion and skill sets surrounding photography and creative content is incredible. There's so much more about Will & Bear than just a hat. The hat is just what makes it all possible.

What does a better world mean to you?

Lauren: To me, it's about people becoming aware of what they consume and the impact that has on both their own lives and the world around them. It's about practising gratitude and awareness and educating ourselves.

Alex: Less environmental destruction and planting more trees.

Do you have any daily rituals?

Lauren: I meditate and exercise before I start each day.

Alex: I'll get out for a surf as much as I can, but exercise in general makes a big difference.

Do you have any mantras?

Lauren: When we started, we'd just dropped a house deposit into the business and were freaking out. Alex said, *"You know what, let's just treat this as an invaluable learning experience. If this fails, we'll have learnt so much."* We keep coming back to this motto; to treat everything as a learning experience.

What does success mean to you?

Alex: Balance - the fine balance of living. And having the space to actually maintain it.

In the world of environmental sustainability, what's an innovative company you'd recommend?

Lauren: Bellroy is one of our favorite brands. We love their stuff. They don't lead with sustainability at their forefront but when you look into them, they're working really hard to do some amazing work and have been for a really long time.

Where do you hope to be five years from now?

Alex: We're hoping to grow further into the US and set up a factory there. We want to be confident and comfortable in our business model first though, so we can replicate it beyond Australia.

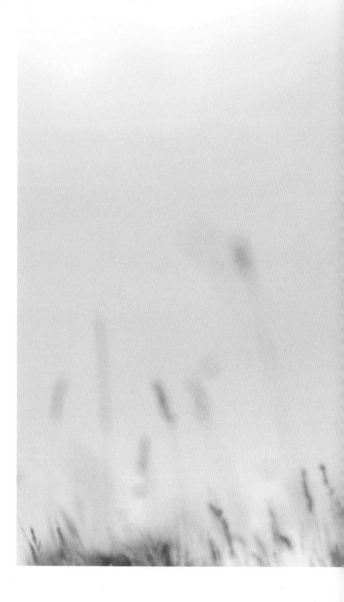

LAUREN WILLIAMS + ALEXANDER KNORR — WILL & BEAR

PAKARAKA PERMACULTURE

PERMACULTURE FARMERS

NIVA + YOTAM KAY

THAMES

How did your past contribute to Pakaraka Permaculture?

Yotam: We met in 2006 during our environmental and peace leadership studies in Israel. Since then, we've been travelling and working in communities around the world on organic farms and studying permaculture. We came to New Zealand seven years ago and are raising our two young girls within this lifestyle, which gives us a lot of pride.

How did the farm come to be?

Niva: After our studies, we both decided the food system was really broken and that learning how to grow food regeneratively is probably one of the most important things we can do, as it affects the whole population. There's also a lot of misunderstanding and conflict within this industry where people think you need to grow large crops with a lot of land, but in our studies we focus on producing more food, of better quality, in more efficient ways - where huge land mass isn't required.

Yotam: We wanted to take the challenge to see how much food we could grow sustainably on a small plot and see how we could make a livelihood from that. We wanted to prove a point in a way - that it can be done - and actually, it has to be done.

> Most soil nowadays is completely depleted and has little to no nutritional value to pass onto the food that's grown in it. That's a real problem.

The size of your garden plays a large part in what you offer, can you explain why?

Yotam: We started this journey not really knowing how much we could accomplish, and now we know - anyone who's willing to put the effort in can do this. For three years in a row now we've grown eight tonnes of produce on a quarter-acre, mainly over the course of seven to eight months of the year, with sales of close to $100,000. We could produce a little bit more with this space if we wanted to but now our focus is more on sharing our many years of learning and experience with other people so they can do it too. We want to see more and more gardens set up to feed communities properly. People can make a living and feed themselves in abundance off of a quarter-acre, and that's amazing compared to the hectares and hectares of chemicals and machinery people usually farm from. It can be done without fungicides, pesticides, herbicides or chemical fertilisers. We grow about twenty-five different commercial crops this way.

> Anything that's cheap is so because someone else has paid the price.

How have you seen the food industry change in recent years?

Yotam: Food is undervalued, it used to be that fifty percent of your salary went into food, whereas now - because food prices have come down, along with the quality — it's only around ten to fifteen percent of people's income. The reason food prices have dropped so much in the last century is because of chemical and petroleum agriculture, which doesn't portray the true price of growing food.

Niva: No one pays for Mother Earth, or even accounts for that cost. People think that organic food is expensive, but it's actually more simply the price of real food. Anything that's cheap is so because someone else has paid the price. In agriculture, it's often the farmers and our soils, our rivers, our air.

How does production on the farm aid environmental sustainability?

Yotam: We've always made living consciously, ethically, organically and with less, our priority in life. Everything we source personally and

professionally is ethical. We'll always choose things that are strong, have a longer life and can be recycled or composted after use, which isn't only environmentally sustainable but also a viable business model. People need to become more aware and be thinking about their choices and the long term. It's largely about where your priorities lie - we don't go out for dinner every week, buy coffees every day or go shopping for new things all the time.

Nothing in life is singular, not even the soil ecology. Everything grows and blooms together.

Niva: We also sell pretty much everything we grow, there's not often a lot that doesn't sell or get eaten at home. When we do have leftovers, we donate them to the Women's Refuge. We also work with soil testing companies to bring the nutritional value of our vegetables up. Our soil is really nutritional now because we've used tonnes of organic high-grade compost, layer upon layer, and we make sure we're continuing to feed those organisms, so they continue to grow. Most soil nowadays is completely depleted and has little to no nutritional value to pass onto the food that's grown in it. That's a real problem.

Are there any standout hardships you've come across?

Yotam: We started this with a really limited budget of just $8000. We bought a few tools and worked full-time. We had to invest back into the business for the first few years before we could see profit, so it's possible, but we recommend people start with a bigger budget if they can so they can reap the benefits of profit sooner and have the critical infrastructure in place so they already know how they're going to achieve their production goals. This is a highly skilled field to be working in, but no different from other skilled professions that people usually put time and money into learning. Anyone who puts the effort in can master it.

What have been some key learning experiences?

Yotam: We learnt by making mistakes a lot of the time. Even though we have a background in this field and a lot of work experience, there was no one around that was doing what we were doing, so at the time it felt like we were forging our own path, which was difficult.

Niva: Our site isn't the perfect space. It's not north facing, it's sloping, and we miss three hours of sunshine each day because of the surrounding forest. We had to learn which months we could grow, as our gardens get heavily shaded in winter, which we had to slow down and which crops would work with our section, things like that. But this is part of the point - if we can do this here, on this site, then people can achieve it everywhere.

Tell us about the rest of the farm?

Yotam: We own the rest of the farm with our neighbours which is 215 acres, including 180 acres of bush. We have sheep, chickens and cattle of all ages living together. We have a food forest with orchards, herbs, flowers, various fruit trees and timber. Our olive orchard has 100 trees which yields 500 litres of olive oil per season, and our chestnut orchard currently yields about two tonnes of nuts each year. Vegetable garden production isn't all we want to do - we're hoping to grow these other areas of trade, but bigger trees and orchards take a lot longer to grow.

You live off the grid here - can you tell us more about that?

Niva: We have five kilowatts of solar panels that we live off, which runs things like our cool room, bread maker, electric car and general household. If we have extra sunlight hours, we use that for our hot water cylinder, and we collect our water from the surrounding mountains. We built a solar cooker (an insulated box that gets to between 80-140 degrees on sunny days) and we use this as a slow cooker outside to make things like rice, chicken, fish, roasts, soups or stews and potatoes. We feed food scraps to our bio-gas digester, which turns scraps into gas and traps it in a big bag that's connected to our stove top. We get our milk, meat and eggs from our cows, sheep and chickens.

What, in your words, is the importance of community?

Niva: Community is very important - *"together we stand, divided we fall"*. Resilience is about community. So much of our contemporary lifestyle is about isolation, to the point where people forget how to speak with one another. I think there's a great desire from within us to have that community and those relationships back. For us, seeing our regular customers and their faces each week at the markets, and how much they appreciate our work, makes it all worth doing - rather than feeling like we're a cog in the system. People in our community are so thankful for what we offer.

We feel we're doing something meaningful. All that we do, our energy and relationship with the garden, is transported over to those people at the markets, who then go and put those carrots in their children's lunch boxes. I think that production line holds a lot of power and positivity, both mentally and physically.

We also have an incredible community of small-scale organic market gardeners (locally, nationally and internationally), which is a huge support. We share ideas, products, equipment, mulch or just progressions and concerns. And that's only the beginning - community runs much deeper than that. Nothing in life is singular, not even the soil ecology. Everything grows and blooms together.

Where do you sell your produce?

We have a great relationship with twelve wholesale restaurants and local stores here and in Auckland - many we've worked with from the very beginning. We also sell fifty percent of our produce at our local farmers' market, and the rest just an hour away in South Auckland.

How is education implemented into your work?

Niva: We have market gardening workshops here on site where we teach people how to set up their own gardens. We want to develop the farm into a living model of agriculture and permaculture, so people can come to stay and have hands-on learning. We also have an online platform of courses for people further away to access, too. We want to share our learnings because the more people who are growing food this way the better, be it in business or just personally in their own backyard.

What, in your words, does permaculture mean?

Yotam: Permaculture is a design system to create habitats. It's about supporting and being a part of natural rhythms. People think it's only about growing, but it's about design as a whole, working with nature to make systems in everything - events, architecture, education. It's about a circular, abundant lifestyle. I consider my vegetable garden and its ecosystem my art.

Niva: What's special about it is its core ethics: earth care, people care and fair share. Anything designed within permaculture has to embody these ethics. It's systematic practices that help, rather than hinder, one another.

If money was no object, what would you do differently?

Yotam: We'd love to create a campus here on site for people to come and stay for our education programme. We aim to do this anyway, but it'll be a much longer process for us to save for it first.

In the world of environmental sustainability, what's an innovative company you'd recommend?

Niva: Thunderpants. We love what they do, their products and the way they collaborate with ethical initiatives.

Where do you hope to be five years from now?

Niva: I think it depends on the state of the world in five years. Each season is becoming more and more challenging. Five years from now, everyone's going to see and understand that we can't go on as we have been.

I think there's a
great desire from
within us to have that
community and those
relationships back.

THE LINE OF SUN
JEWELLER

ALICE TSAKIRAKIS

MELBOURNE

How did The Line of Sun come to be?

I studied a Bachelor of Design and worked as a textile designer for many years before starting The Line of Sun. It was initially a 'just for fun' kind of project with my husband. We wanted to share a creative outlet together and decided on making jewellery just to be able to make pieces for our friends and ourselves. My job at the time involved a lot of staring at a computer screen, so working with my hands was such a refreshing break from that. I was immediately obsessed with the freedom and craftsmanship of sculpting jewellery and very quickly I knew it was what I wanted to do full-time.

What did you set out to achieve?

Initially, I never had big plans for what I wanted to achieve as a brand, it was more about pursuing an interest and pushing myself in an area I knew nothing about. But my underlying vision has always been the same - creating quality pieces locally, that are designed to last, without sacrificing the world around us. The style of my pieces has somewhat evolved over time as I've improved my skills, but it's always been very handmade, intentionally textured and imperfect.

How has the company grown?

It's been about seven years since I first started experimenting with making jewellery, but only two years since I really went for it as a career rather than a hobby. It's grown very organically as I was never driven to become a big brand, it's been more about exploring the medium and how to run a business, so there's lots of learning curves along the way.

Like any small business, there's been lots of ups and downs and a whole lot of hard work. The first few years were slow when it was just a side project. Since we had our first child and I decided to focus on it full-time, there's been really nice, steady growth. Now it's more about managing that growth so I can maintain the balance between my work and family.

Are there any standout hardships you've come across?

Financially, the first few years were tough. I left a really secure, well-paying job and whilst I've always had a lot of great support around me, it's still pretty daunting. I'm confident on the creative side of things, but learning all the logistics of running a business has taken a while to get my head around.

I have to keep trying not to be too hard on myself and understand that I'm in a constant state of growth and evolution.

What have been some key learning experiences?

There's been lot! For a while, I felt like I had to come across like I was really established by pretending I had a big team behind me - which makes me laugh so much now. I think I dropped a lot of that ego after having children and now really pride myself on the fact that everything is run by me. Staying true to myself and not feeling like I *have* to produce more because customers or stores are asking for it has been a valuable lesson. I now put out smaller collections in my own time, when the inspiration strikes. This way everything feels really genuine and I'm confident and in love with every single piece.

> I felt like I had to come across like I was really established by pretending I had a big team behind me – and now really pride myself on the fact that everything is run by me.

Can you explain the difference between your production process and that of regular jewellery on the market?

There are so many differences, I don't know where to start. Firstly, most big brands design pieces in CAD (computer aided design) then send those designs offshore and produce them in huge quantities, using cheap base metals.

WILD KINSHIP — CONVERSATIONS WITH CONSCIOUS ENTREPRENEURS

Ranges are often produced in high frequency and then go to sale at the end of the season.

In contrast, I carve all of my pieces by hand in wax, and then cast very small quantities in Melbourne. As everything is made locally, I can make pieces to order - meaning I don't have excess product waste or excess stock. I use either a sterling silver base metal or solid gold, metals that can be infinitely recycled, so all of my metal scraps are refined and used again and again. I aim to make pieces that are timeless in design rather than trend driven, so I don't need to design to the typical fashion seasons. I have a maximum of two ranges a year and will keep the styles on range for as long as I feel like making them. All of this ensures I have a really minimal and streamlined business.

You work with the method of lost wax casting - can you explain this technique?

Lost wax casting is an ancient jewellery making technique. I start with a block of jeweller's wax, and using an array of tools like files, sandpaper and a flame, I slowly carve and melt the wax into the desired shape, which is then cast in precious metals.

What, in your words, is the importance of ethical manufacturing and sourcing of materials?

My strong ethics are what drove me to start my own business in the first place. After working for large companies producing pieces in the thousands, with very little regard to the implications of that process, I became really disgusted by the industry. So, when I started out, I knew that being an ethical business that was completely transparent was paramount. Since day one I've had this in the forefront of my mind, so it's not even a conscious thought process now - I can't imagine running a business any other way.

How do you find work life balance with a young family?

It's definitely a delicate balance. I think most mums running a business with small children would agree that it can be really hard. My studio went from this lovely shared workspace with other incredible artists to my son, Leroy's bedroom...while he naps in our room! It's the reality of working from home, although obviously a short-term solution.

I think it takes a lot of patience and I'm still learning that I have to just go with the flow. There are some weeks where I have so much work on

and client appointments, then the kids get sick and I have to cancel everything. But the reason I wanted to work for myself in the first place was to be able to have that flexibility and to be able to be with my boys when they need me.

Some advice to mothers considering starting a business - you need to be 110 percent committed to the journey. If you're not completely in it, or in it for the wrong reasons, then you'll never be able to stick it out. It's not easy, but the hard times are definitely outweighed by the joy of being able to spend quality time with your babies whenever they need you.

We have a much slower pace in our household, and I wouldn't trade that for the world.

What does a better world mean to you?

Less stuff, and people buying things of quality that last longer. We've become so accustomed to the thrill of cheap purchases with the mindset of constantly discarding and repurchasing. I really hope this shifts and society rediscovers the joy of living a life more simply.

What, in your eyes, is the company's biggest success?

Staying true to my vision of staying a locally made brand with a strong conscience.

What would be your biggest sacrifice in running a small business?

If I'd stayed on my old career path, we'd definitely be better off financially. That sacrifice can be hard sometimes but running my own business has given me so much more than I could've ever imagined. I work part-time, and the days I'm working I make sure I spend a few hours with my boys in the morning rather than rushing out the door. We have a much slower pace in our household, and I wouldn't trade that for the world.

How does environmental sustainability spill into your personal life?

We live very simply. We hardly buy new clothes, and when we do, they're quality staples that will last many years to come. My husband is a furniture maker so he either makes pieces for our home or we buy second-hand, and he repairs them.

It's really important to us that our children grow up with a love for our environment and a great sense of imagination, so a lot of playtime is focused on repurposing recycled materials and pieces we find in nature, rather than buying new toys. It's not so much a conscious decision anymore, it's just our lifestyle and we want our children to understand you don't need things to make you happy.

Who's your biggest inspiration?

There are too many to mention, but my number one is always Frida Kahlo. Her resilience throughout her hardships is something that inspires me every day.

Do you live by any mantra?

Own who you are.

What does success mean to you?

Living on my own terms.

Where do you hope to be five years from now?

To be honest, I hope to be in much the same spot as I am now. I'm really lucky to have experienced the growth I have in a short amount of time, and even though I'm constantly brimming with ideas, I need to keep reminding myself to slow down and enjoy the process. So, I'll continue to manage my growth and ensure each piece is made with purpose while prioritising the natural environment around me.

...we want our children to understand you don't need things to make you happy.

LE WORKSHOP
TINY HOMES

SARAH-LEE + FRANÇOIS GUITTÉNIT

NAPIER

How did your past contribute to Le Workshop?

François: We started Le Workshop when we moved to Hawke's Bay about six years ago. I'm a cabinetmaker by trade, so we started out doing custom-made furniture and cabinetry, which naturally evolved into our tiny homes business. We'd just bought this land for the workshop and had been renting a house when we had to move out. We decided to be resourceful and use the land instead of getting into debt buying elsewhere, so we built ourselves a tiny home to live in. I'd been working on building sites since I was fifteen back home in France, so we designed something that suited our family and went for it.

> To me, money is a tool, but it's not what gets me out of bed in the morning. There has to be passion there for that.

Sarah-Lee: We've always thought within a holistic, creative, design mentality, and through much of our relationship, even in the early days, we'd sit around drawing up different plans for houses or campers or teepees, just for fun. François and I met while he was travelling New Zealand on a surf trip. He was living in a van and we'd both just come out of our studies that had a design basis. We were both in this passion-driven, creative space where the world was our oyster and we were instantly attracted to those qualities in one another. We started talking about design and have never really stopped, thirteen years later.

We loved living in Auckland in our twenties but found we were growing out of the big city life, so opted for a slower, simpler existence. We moved to a friend's land out in Mangawhai and converted a bus into a house with our first baby, Poppy. We lived there, off the grid, between the bus and a cabin for a year. We never set out to be tiny house designers as a profession - we just didn't want to sign up to a mortgage for the next thirty years.

How did the idea of tiny homes evolve into a business?

Sarah-Lee: It's become so common to live with a mortgage, but it's incredibly limiting and really dictates your life. So, when we had to move out of our rental in Hawke's Bay, we wanted an option that wouldn't limit us in that way, especially with a young family. We both wanted the freedom to be at home with the kids and have a big impact on their lives, rather than be too stressed and too busy with work, just so we can pay the bank for our shelter.

François: Because of the location of our tiny house and workshop (within suburbia but close to the beach), people could see our house and would always stop to check it out. Often tiny homes are way up in the hills or off the grid, so people don't see them. It was the exposure that really made the project evolve into the business it is. People started asking us to build them one, and then another, and that just continued to flow.

What have been some key learning experiences?

François: It's important to understand there's going to be ups and downs within business. It can and will be hard, but you can't throw in the towel every time it gets difficult. It's not smooth sailing but it's worth it in the long run.

People put a lot of pressure on their careers, but I don't think it really matters what you're doing as long as there's passion there - you'll learn everything you need to and you stop counting the hours and do it for love. People are often intimidated or too afraid to chase their passions or change their careers to something they really love and get excited about. To me, money is a tool, but it's not what gets me out of bed in the morning. There has to be passion there for that.

Can you talk us through the build process?

We do all of the design drawings and build specifications and each build takes roughly six weeks. There are no real set plans, we sit down with each client and talk about their needs, how they connect and use a space and how we can reflect these values within the design.

How do you find living in a tiny home with a growing family?

Sarah-Lee: We love living a home-based life where we also work and our children learn from. We have three children under eleven, plus our dog Georgie, and for now it works! We don't really believe there's one house that will get you through every season of life. These things are always changing and evolving as we grow. So, it's not forever but right now the pros far outweigh the cons. We believe a home should offer a place of rest and respite: of centring and being.

We also live a much more connected, present life as a family; it's not the kids in that room and the parents down the other end of the house. We're very engaged in one another's lives and if there's a problem, we face it head on and resolve it, because we have to. We feel those are great life lessons and coping mechanisms to be implementing in our children's lives. There's no carpet to sweep issues under or doors to slam, so it becomes a very open, honest, close relationship.

In what ways does your production process aid the environment?

François: Our tiny homes are built around steel framing on a trailer that's engineered locally. We use a recycled sheep wool blend made from carpet waste for insulation, similar to Pink Batts, which is also less allergenic. Our exterior cladding is largely made up of New Zealand grown cedar, with poplar ply internally. The poplar's light colouring helps to make smaller spaces look bigger and is a more sustainable fast-growing timber that there's an abundance of.

Our windows are all double-glazed, low E, argon-filled with timber cedar frames, which helps hugely with heat sealing and transfer in comparison with your usual aluminium frames. We build all our wooden window frames and source the glass locally and use natural flaxseed fibre flooring and resins with no VOCs. There's little within the build that's sourced internationally or has a transport footprint. The biggest energy user in the house is the fridge. Our power bill is around twenty dollars a month year-round for a family of five, home full-time.

Waste within the standard building industry is huge.

So much of it could be avoided with a little forward planning and better design, but instead, good quality materials often go to landfill. Because we build onsite and we're working with the same materials repeatedly, it's easier for us to reuse and recycle all of our offcuts. We're mindful in all we do - right down to putting our unused wood chips on the side of the road for people to use in their gardens.

Our houses are more cost effective to build, more efficient to run, have less maintenance and don't cost the planet with their production or over their lifetime. It's a beautiful way to simplify your life financially and leave more time for quality moments spent with loved ones, passion projects and adventure.

> We live a much more connected, present life as a family. There's no carpet to sweep issues under or doors to slam, so it becomes a very open, honest, close relationship.

How does environmental sustainability spill into your personal lives?

Sarah-Lee: We're very connected and aware across all areas of our lives, which naturally begets environmental sustainability. Our choices become our habits, our habits become our character, and our character is who we are and what our life is. Life is just a sum of all our choices, be it financial, emotional, physical or spiritual. Likewise, every time you buy something, you're casting a vote for who you want to support and become, which has a huge influence on your footprint.

What does a better world mean to you?

François: If everyone was focused on making the world better for the next generation. We're all imperfect, and as we grow older, we start to learn from our mistakes and see those imperfections, so if we could pass those lessons on to the youth around us and really make their benefit our focus, the world would quickly become a better place.

We can't keep up the rat race and push the kids aside because we don't have time, then expect them to be better or the result to be different.

Do you have any daily rituals?

Sarah-Lee: I'm an early riser and spend that time centring myself and setting my day's intention, then it's time for coffee.

François: I wake up to the sound of Sarah-Lee placing my coffee on the mezzanine at my head. We enjoy a coffee together and then the kids climb up to join us in our bed one by one. We are intentional in maintaining morning rhythms which are peaceful and present.

In the world of environmental sustainability, what's an innovative company you'd recommend?

Sarah-Lee: I love the impact Ecostore has had on our sustainable landscape in New Zealand. They've broken into the mainstream and introduced synthetic chemical free and plastic free to the masses. The power of change is in the unity, and they've nailed it.

Where do you hope to be five years from now?

François: We definitely want to be living on a lifestyle block with more trees and space and less traffic. We'd like to do some mission trips overseas with the children so they can see the world past New Zealand - we have a goal to do five continents in five years with the kids. Professionally, who knows? We have lots of ideas and projects that we'll do one day. We love what we're doing but we try not to become personally attached to it. We want the freedom to continue to let life ebb and flow and see where it takes us.

...every time you buy something, you're casting a vote for who you want to support and become.

SARAH-LEE+ FRANÇOIS GUITTENIT — LE WORKSHOP

LOCO LOVE
CHOCOLATES

EMICA PENKLIS + JESSE LAWRENCE

BYRON BAY

How did Loco Love come to be?

Emica: I was working as a naturopath in a dispensary in Sydney when a customer approached me to formulate some chocolate recipes. It really took on its own life after that. I didn't have any business experience so it's been a pretty steep learning curve, but I guess I didn't take it very seriously for the first few years. I was still travelling and just doing it on the side. I started making the chocolates at home and then rented a space in friends' commercial kitchens which really helped Loco Love to bloom in those early days, although it wasn't until we got our own factory that things really took off.

Jesse: I'd been working in architecture and then met Emica and we started working together. I found a bunch of stockists to start selling the chocolates and we got a tiny kitchen space within a warehouse in Ballina to work from; we pretty much just lived in this dingy little kitchen, working all the time. Now we have our own factory in Byron that's a custom fit-out and is amazing.

> It was quite a transitional time in my life in general, I'd started meditating and had this perspective shift on the world around me at the same time as forming the company, which really pulled me from this sort of depression that I'd been in previously.

Emica: Having a real base to work from has really helped with the growth of the company and our own creativity.

How has the company grown?

Emica: We've been running for about seven years now, but it's mostly developed in the past few years, especially since we took on the new factory in Byron and developed gorgeous shelf stable packaging. We have about 400 stockists within Australia and then a few scattered across the US, France, Canada and New Zealand.

What's the ethos behind the brand?

Emica: I've always loved to make and create things. Chocolate became a great catalyst for this, which incorporated naturopathy because of the herbs I was using. The 'love' part came from a really personal space and the journey of finding fulfilment, gratitude and happiness in going out on my own and creating this company that brought me so much joy. It was quite a transitional time in my life in general, I'd started meditating and had this perspective shift on the world around me at the same time as forming the company, which really pulled me from this sort of depression that I'd been in previously. I think if we can all find that loving space within ourselves, we'll be kinder, better people in the world.

Because of this, I wanted the chocolate to be a sort of meditation where you can be in the moment and tap into that energy.

Are there any standout hardships you've come across?

Jesse: Byron is a really transient town and people often come here to have a good time, surf, travel and enjoy their freedom so it can be hard to get long-term staff that are passionate about our ethos, as well as hardworking, committed and have that attention to detail. Being really inexperienced within the world of business has also meant we've really had to learn each stage as we've gone along. Things could've been easier if we had a bit of business experience behind us initially.

Emica: Trying to find a balance with work and personal life is hard, too. I started Loco Love out of positive energy for this new lease on life where I'd implemented set routines and morning rituals, but it's been difficult to hold on to these important practices as the business has grown.

What have been some key learning experiences?

Emica: Learning to seek and ask for professional help. You have to be pretty obsessed with what you're doing - it's hard, so you have to have the love to really stick at it. With our first baby on the way, it's definitely making us change our perspective and re-evaluate what's important going forward within the business. It might end up being a blessing in disguise, although it's a little overwhelming now working out how we're going to juggle everything.

What's been your biggest sacrifice in running Loco Love?

Jesse: Self-care and time with friends and family. We also have this real guilt around not working, so it's hard to switch off and stop. We do love it though, at the end of the day I'm not sure I would call it a sacrifice because we'd choose this option every day.

> You have to be pretty obsessed with what you're doing - it's hard, so you have to have the love to really stick at it.

How does your production process differ from that of regular chocolate brands on the market?

Emica: We're super hands on. We grind all the fillings, activate all the nuts, dehydrate the berries and make every ingredient. Like our hazelnut paste - we make it from scratch rather than buying it. There's a lot of energy and intention within every single piece. We don't use things like sweeteners, sugars and stabilisers, so the ingredients and manufacturing conditions need to be perfect. We also have little waste, we probably only fill one bag a week at the factory which we're really mindful of.

Jesse: We're very aware of where we're sourcing our ingredients from and have relationships with most of our suppliers, so we know the products are organic and high quality. We also try to source locally and fair trade wherever possible. It's a really lengthy process to create our chocolates, and because of the quality ingredients and herbs used within them, our margins are really small. Having those small margins means we have to continue to be super hands on in every aspect of the business because we can't afford to outsource as much.

The chocolates are really unique recipes, some which have taken us two years or more to develop, so we hold them really close to heart.

Can you tell us about the addition of herbs and the benefits they offer?

We use a lot of different herbs within our chocolates. The medicinal mushrooms are amazing because they're good for so many different areas of health. We use Reishi for the immune system and calmness, He Shou Wu for anti-ageing and mood, Schisandra for liver health, increased energy and blood flow, and Lion's Mane which is good for the nervous system and helps focus. We're also working on releasing a hot chocolate powder with medicinal mushrooms soon which we're really excited about, we've been recipe testing and sourcing really incredible organic medicinal mushrooms that have been scientifically analysed for active constituents.

You work with B1G1 - can you explain this relationship?

Jesse: We wanted to find a way to give back. B1G1 is essentially about business for good. We make donations to their not-for-profit organisation and choose which charity we want to support, from helping kids in Africa, planting a tree or working to fight sex trafficking. They work with thousands of different charities across the world and really vet them to make sure all the money is going where it's needed.

What are your biggest passions beyond Loco Love?

Emica: Writing, exploring the human psyche in a way that draws inspiration from great alchemists, such as Hermes Trismegistus and spirituality through meditation and nature.

Jesse: Surfing and playing guitar. I also enjoy building and using my hands.

What, in your eyes, is the company's biggest success?

Emica: We get a lot of really positive, and often quite moving, feedback from people who have resonated with our ethos. It's really impacted some of their lives which is pretty special. For me, this product was a sort of saving grace so it's amazing to hear it's been able to do the same thing for others in their own way.

What does a better world mean to you?

Emica: A more compassionate world with less greed, where people can take responsibility for their own actions. We're creating our own reality, but as a collective, we place blame on everything else.

Jesse: From me, it's where people are open to more love.

Who's your biggest inspiration?

Emica: Nature. I'm not sure it would be another person. Inspiration comes from spirit.

Do you live by any mantra?

Jesse: Be present.

In the world of environmental sustainability, what's an innovative company you'd recommend?

Jesse: Patagonia.

Emica: Any company that is conscious of their waste, their effect on human happiness and environmental sustainability is better, but as a world we still have a really long way to go.

Where do you hope to be five years from now?

Emica: Retired? No, but seriously - working less, having more time for painting, writing and meditating.

Jesse: Hopefully having a lot more freedom for family, surfing and simple pleasures.

KOWTOW
WOMENSWEAR

GOSIA PIATEK

WELLINGTON

How did Kowtow come to be?

I started the business with no real fashion experience. I was just working odd jobs here and there - going snowboarding and having fun was my main focus. But I got to the point where I felt I needed to get stuck into something real and start a career for myself. Back then, the Labour government was giving away grants to small business startups, which was amazing. They also taught you how to write a business plan, which was invaluable advice often missed nowadays. I think I did five different plans right off the bat, all in different fields, but in the end decided to keep it simple with t-shirts. A friend of mine suggested I start a fair trade organic cotton fabric brand, and honestly at that stage I didn't even know what that was! But I became really obsessed the more I researched it. I love nature and I knew I wanted to do something that protected it. I thought it was really cool how you could be totally transparent in your entire production train by using a certified fair trade labelling organisation, too. From there, one thing led to another and the business started to find its roots.

How would you best summarise your offering?

Our ranges are made from certified ethical and sustainable fibres. Currently we are inspired by colour and volume. We work very hard to always improve what we are doing as times change and new sustainable technologies come about. It is very important for us to be progressive and to always embrace new ideas.

What did you set out to achieve?

What I think is really cool is showing people that you can be an environmentally friendly and ethical business, and still be profitable. The two can go hand in hand. This is where I started out - I wanted to prove to people that you can do both, and on an international level.

We've gotten to a point now where we're completely circular with our packaging. We use cornstarch bags which get sent to an industrial composter in Auckland where they're composted with organic matter and distributed around local orchards. We tried lots of alternative options but found problems with them, like the waste being sent offshore to other countries to be processed, which didn't make any sense to me. We wanted to find a way to stop, go back and work out our own option that was better, so we just made calls and did research and found a guy that could do it.

There's always a way. People put all of these roadblocks in place or think it's too hard but there are plenty of options out there, you just have to find them. It doesn't have to be some big company, either. It can be someone in your community that could benefit from it, too.

> Information, accessibility and options are always evolving and so we have to move with it when we can. As the population continues to grow, and as this wash up of plastic continues to occur, we all really need to be taking responsibility and changing our ways.

How has the company grown?

The company has been running for thirteen years now, and a lot has changed in this time. When I first started out, sustainability in general was a bit of a weird, out there concept, whereas now it's become the new-age luxury.

We've always been a self-funded business, so we've never taken out loans. Everything has grown organically within the company from demand. We're now a team of thirty staff and we have warehousing in America, Europe and Australia, plus sales offices

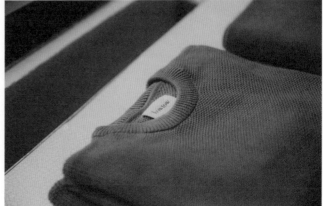

in London, Melbourne and here in New Zealand.

Are there any standout hardships you've come across?

It took me roughly eight months of initial research to find the growers and manufacturers that I wanted to work with, so it was quite difficult. The industry was so small at that time. The farms we work with in India are very different to those in America, they're really small-scale farmers who only have one to two acres of land that they live on, so they're far more in tune with what's going on. They're also far more affected by what they put on their land, which impacts their output.

Since those initial foundations, hardships within the business? None really, which I feel a little bit guilty saying. I have an amazing team who handle the business. I'm living in London part of the year with my partner, and I can go away and come back knowing things are better than when I left. I guess because we started off with such strong values, amazing people were drawn to us and they're really engaged. I don't have to keep tabs on them and make sure they're doing their work or turning up on time because they're genuinely invested and really care about what we're doing here. They want to be here. People are probably the hardest thing to manage, but our team is really empathetic and compassionate, so we work well together.

I guess I've had some personal hardships. I fell in love with a guy in England and we had a baby really quickly. I was used to being here in Wellington, managing my business, and then I was suddenly away from it which was hard for my micromanagement self - but it actually made the business better. It means I've had to pull away. I don't think we'd be here, with this much growth, if that hadn't happened. I'd have still been stuck in the details. I remember swing-tagging the clothes until three in the morning, whereas this way I just had to let other people help.

What have been some key learning experiences?

Letting ago and trusting in your team. It can feel completely counter-intuitive to let go, but it's so important for growth and sustainability of the business.

I have a commerce degree and I'm really big on financial reviews and keeping tabs on our growth. I guess that's partly because my parents didn't come

from money - we came to New Zealand as refugees from Poland. My parents are amazing and very well educated, so they got good jobs early on. My mum can make something out of nothing, and she doesn't take anything for granted. Every little piece of food was used in our house, nothing ever went to waste. People who throw food away, I simply think they're crazy. The amount of work it took to grow, make, harvest, package, ship and buy, and then to just throw it out? I don't understand it.

> ## Letting ago and trusting in your team. It can feel completely counter-intuitive to let go, but it's so important for growth and sustainability of the business.

So, I probably learnt a lot from them when it comes to money and running a business. I try to instill the value of the product and its whole lifecycle in my staff, too. I encourage them not to take things for granted, and to be resourceful and mindful.

Can you explain the difference between your production process and that of fast fashion labels on the market?

I have no idea what a fast fashion brand does. But we design from yarn, which I think is completely different to other brands. Most people buy their fabric off the roll but then they don't know where the fabric has come from. Most of it can't be traced back to the farm level. Whereas we work with the farmers and secure the raw cotton eighteen months in advance, then we create the yarn ourselves and develop it from there. I actually didn't realise initially that this wasn't the norm. So, because of this lengthy production process, we're actually working a season ahead of everyone else which means we don't tend to look at trends as much. Instead, we forecast on what we're vibing off and what's working for us, or what direction we want to be moving into. Fast fashion brands would never be able to work with that sort of lead time, it's way too long.

We also sea freight and pack everything in biodegradable packaging. We have a circularity programme so everything, including our back-neck labels, are made from organic cotton. Our buttons are made from recycled hemp in Italy, and we use metal (nickel-free) tacks on our denim that are made in Germany. We offer a free repair programme in store, too, so any Kowtow piece - no matter how long you've owed it – we'll repair for free if required.

We've only ever worked with two factories - one of them for thirteen years - and we have really great relationships with them. If the price of cotton goes up, because they might not have had the same rainfall and crop that year, we don't just replace our factory and go elsewhere. And we don't go to six different factories with a style and see who can do it cheapest, which is really common of fast fashion labels.

Can you talk us through the production process of organic clothing?

Cotton, for example, is really complex. It goes through a lot of different stages in an in-depth production chain. It has to be grown, and because each piece of cotton has seeds in it, it goes through a machine that takes the lint away from the seed. Then the lint has to be spun into a yarn, before it can be woven or knitted, then dyed. This is why when you see super cheap clothing, like five-dollar t-shirts and fifteen-dollar dresses, you have to think about how that item of clothing came to be and understand that within the production line, something's getting missed. It's usually the quality and the labour. It's impossible to make ethical, non-synthetic garments for those prices.

How can the fashion industry negatively impact us, both socially and environmentally?

A huge example of this is that there are ten thousand farmer suicides a year in India alone. Conventional cotton is grown with pesticides, and initially the farmers get an amazing crop, but the land requires more and more pesticides as the years go on and it becomes completely reliant on them, which perpetuates a cycle of debt with the farmers and pesticide companies. It usually gets to the point where the pesticide companies will give them a loan because they now need this product, but it has an interest rate, so farmers are stuck in debt with a worsening product, gaining more debt. Farmers have started drinking the poison

because they just can't cope. Instead, these farmers could just be planting two rows of lentils that will also provide food for their families, like they do on our farms, and then a row of cotton which gives the soil nitrogen and helps with their crops. When things are companion planted, we can see amazing results that don't require synthetic fertiliser.

What does a better world mean to you?

No new plastic - shame on us humans. Living in more harmony with nature, even though that sounds so cheesy. And maybe being more in touch and human in our contact. Finding ways for positive outcomes that are not driven by corporate greed.

I think it's the designer's responsibility to take care of the end result of their product.

Have you noticed a rise in awareness of environmental sustainability?

I think people are now starting to understand the concept a lot more, so we can actually start talking about it as a company, too. But there's also a lot of 'greenwashing' out there so you need to educate yourself as a consumer. We're really geeky with our information and want to be thorough in our transparency, what we offer and how we educate people. These are not easy subjects; they can be overwhelming. So, we try to make the information really simple and digestible for the consumer so they can understand and trust us and make informed decisions.

What, to you, is the company's biggest success?

The size that we've grown to with the products we have, and seeing the whole thing work while being able to stay true to our values the whole time. Having international recognition is pretty amazing as well. If I look back to the first day I started this company, I never would've thought we'd be where we are now. And those values are only strengthening and being instilled further.

What would be your biggest sacrifice in running a small business?

My family time. Because my partner lives in London, and my son and I go between, we miss out on a lot of family time which can be hard. In saying that, now I'm not sure I'd fit into that normal life again – I'm so used to how it is. But more time to reconnect would be nice. To put that in perspective though, I'm just having a middle-class whine. Loads of people spend lots of time apart for worse reasons.

What are your biggest passions beyond Kowtow?

I think if I didn't have Kowtow I'd definitely be doing environmental work, maybe not in fashion, but some sort of design.

Who's your biggest inspiration?

I don't really have a muse. But I follow loads of activists and grassroots organisations and am into people like Jane Goodall more than anything.

In the world of environmental sustainability, what's an innovative company you'd recommend?

I don't know if I have a specific company, but I really love supporting cultural arts and crafts. There's a beauty in slowing things down and using methods that are hundreds of years old. The idea that you don't need to be continuously reinventing yourself is really nice.

Where do you hope to be five years from now?

I'd love to see standalone Kowtow stores all over the world, and to be stronger in our international presence. Collaborating with some amazing designers who have the same ethics, like a shoe designer or something, would be cool. And for me personally - to have a little more stability and presence in my personal life, whether that's here or in London.

ORCHARD ST.
PLANT MEDICINES + ELIXIR BARS

KIRSTEN SHANKS

SYDNEY

How did Orchard St. come to be?

I'd been working as a naturopath for nearly seven years before Orchard St. I've always been captivated by herbal medicine and biology - the study of life, it really resonates with me. It was during my naturopathic studies that I started to create a much deeper relationship with and understanding of the plant kingdom. I'd opened a clinic in Australia and was working there when my mum went through a battle with cancer. I dropped everything, closed the clinic and went home to Christchurch to be with her.

After my time back in New Zealand, I moved to New York to be with my now-husband, James. I was struggling a little bit within myself after caring for my mother through that difficult period of her life and didn't feel the pull towards treating patients in a purely clinical setting anymore. I felt I needed a change and spent much of my time in New York delving into a variety of different spiritual studies.

The cold pressed juice and raw food movement was blowing up in New York at the time, which inspired the beginnings of Orchard St. I loved the idea of sharing and integrating plant medicines into something as accessible as juice. I wanted to find a way that I could create a more holistic cleanse experience, one that would take people on a deeper wellness journey. For a lot of people, a green juice is just that - but often it's where their journey begins.

> ...taking on a team and allowing yourself to step back is how you grow.

How has the company grown?

Initially, we launched online as a juice cleanse business incorporating plant medicines and

native botanicals throughout. It really took off, we were living in an apartment and making everything there from dawn to dusk - the garage and fridges were overflowing. Within a month, we had to lease a commercial kitchen and from there I opened our Bronte store, which was more of a storefront for my naturopathy clinic and dispensary with a little juice fridge.

Our Bondi and Paddington stores came about a year later as Elixir Bars, which gave me a real opportunity to weave plant medicines into food and drink in this delicious and accessible way, and in a really connected space.

We now produce 100 different plant medicine products, plus the food and juices. Then we have the clinics and dispensary. I have limitless inspiration and have ten different creations and ideas on the go at any one time, so it's quite busy, but I have an amazing team and support system. We really are a collective sum of our parts, working together. We've been running for just over six years now, and although I absolutely drive it creatively and experientially, my team are the ones who really hold the space day-to-day.

Are the any standout hardships you've come across?

Oh of course, where do I start? In the early days, and before I became a mum, I just worked every moment of every day – you're just so driven you don't even question it until six months pass. I literally didn't have a day off for seven or eight months. After that, I had a bit of a crash and burn which made me reassess and take on more support. Which is a really important lesson: taking on a team and allowing yourself to step back is how you grow.

When my son Sonny came along three years ago, I had to do that again - reassess and find a new way to make it work. During that time, we went through some big changes within the business mechanics behind the scenes, so it was a period of change and uncertainty. I had to decide whether to call it or push forward, which of course can come at great sacrifice. I never wanted to let go, I knew the potential Orchard St. had to make true change in the world and there was so much love invested, it was just about finding a way to keep moving forward.

What, in your words, is the importance of community?

I never wanted the business to be about me, it was

always about our offering and inspiring a greater connection to these plant medicines, to this earth. I really hid behind the scenes for the first few years, but I came to learn that your relationship with your community is what binds you to this hub of incredible people. And that's what Orchard St. is all about; creating this space for people to explore and journey through. Each store has its own demographic and community, based around their own lifestyle, which is important to nurture.

What, to you, is the importance of supporting nature's rhythms?

Plant medicines have been used forever. Our ancestors had such a deeply connected, intuitive relationship and respect for this land; their lives revolved around it, from their food to their sacred medicine. Everything was about this notion of nurturing and honouring Mother Earth, working with her to create an abundance to live off. A reciprocal relationship. Over the years, societies have completely lost touch with this and used our planet for our own gain, which has resulted in so much damage. It's only now that we're really seeing the cost of that damage so widely and are beginning to understand why treating her with utmost reverence, as sacred, is essential for our future.

How do you find work life balance with a young family?

This was a really big adjustment for me. Before Sonny was born, I'd always envisioned myself as this really nurturing, present mother that would spend every moment of every day on the floor doing arts and crafts or out in nature singing Steiner songs. But I also thought that I'd have him strapped onto my chest and carry on with my daily rituals and workflow. Somehow it didn't occur to me you can't do both all of the time! Surrendering to that, learning how to nurture both parts of my life separately, and together, was a juggle. More than anything little ones teach you to slow down. They teach you what really matters.

What does a better world mean to you?

Written on Sonny's wall we have a quote, *"In a world where you can be anything, be kind."* Kindness and compassion, to me, is everything. Kindness for ourselves, for Mother Earth, for the people around us. A better world ultimately is where we return to a deep reverence for our Earth. It's become so lost over the years, we've had some incredible advances,

sure, but in that we've also lost that relationship and respect that honours her. Orchard St. is my way to connect and devote myself to that cause.

What, to you, is the company's biggest success?

The communities that have grown around the business. The lives that have been touched. And, internally within my team, the people it has brought together. I know that many lives have been positively influenced, in one way or another, because of Orchard St.

Do you have any daily rituals?

A meditation practice. I started diving into spirituality when I was really young so have dipped into many different forms of meditation over the years. For me, my escape mechanism when the going gets hard is to vacate. I don't find it hard to transcend, so a more embodied practice where I'm being fully present in the experience is more beneficial for me. I also have a tea practice that's deeply meditative to me, and honours the plant kingdom. I do a bit of a qi gong influenced yoga flow too, and often dance, just whatever I can fit in before Sonny wakes in the morning.

What's your go-to when you're in a creative rut?

When I'm caught up with the paperwork of running a business, I really just need to get back to nature. I dive into the ocean, go for a walk, head to the farm, reconnect and slow down.

In the world of environmental sustainability, what's an innovative company you'd recommend and why?

Organisations like the Australian Conservation Society come to mind, rather than a specific business. The work they do is really incredible.

Where do you hope to be five years from now?

I hope to be a greater resource for education in the future. Not simply the offerings, but the tools for empowerment as well. While I have a very clear vision of our future, you can never really be sure exactly how things will evolve, only that they will as the time is right.

KIRSTEN SHANKS — ORCHARD ST.

Everything was about this notion of nurturing and honouring Mother Earth, working with her to create an abundance to live off. A reciprocal relationship. Over the years, societies have completely lost touch with this and used our planet for our own gain, which has resulted in so much damage. It's only now that we're really seeing the cost of that damage so widely and are beginning to understand why treating her with utmost reverence, as sacred, is essential for our future.

VICTORIA AGUIRRE + CARL WILSON

BYRON BAY

How did Pampa come to be?

Victoria: Carl and I met in Chile a little over seven years ago; he was there on a surf trip travelling all over South America. I am from Argentina, but I was working as a journalist writing a travel story on what to do in Chile. Carl was developing his passion for photography then, so we instantly connected. We travelled together around South America for three months, living the simple life with lots of camping and surfing. He asked me to come to Australia with him, so we went back to live on the Gold Coast together. Carl went back to his trade as an air-conditioning mechanic.

I found the move to Australia quite difficult - I didn't have a visa to work properly and became quite depressed and a little lost having left everything behind with no real plan forward. I hit a really dark moment and needed to make a change and find a way out. It was through this sadness that Pampa was born. Pampa means 'fertile earth'. It's a very normal and common word to use in Latin America and it's also a place near where I grew up. I thought if I wanted to stay here in Australia, I had to find something that connected me to my roots and my home. So, I started asking myself what makes me thrive, what makes me warm and happy again and what defines my home of Latin America to me.

Because of this, the brand really came before the product. I had a really strong sense of what I wanted the brand to be, so we set about finding a product to match.

How did you begin sourcing your products?

Victoria: Carl wasn't very happy back in his trade after our year of travel, so we went back to South America together and started searching for artisans. It was quite difficult to get away from the typical commercial products, so we kept going deeper and deeper into the mountains and literally started knocking on doors until we found the pieces that we fell in love with. We came back to Australia with a few rugs but were quite naive and not sure how to really launch it from there. It was so new at that time, no one was doing anything so authentically South American in Australia. Over time, we've built up a big extended family of makers.

> I hit a really dark moment and needed to make a change and find a way out. It was through this sadness that Pampa was born.

How has the company grown?

Victoria: We've been running for a little over seven years now. We launched our brand through a beautiful interior design store in Sydney and were doing wholesale initially, but found that, because of the quality of the products we were sourcing, there wasn't a lot of room for a real margin. We became really selective with who we stocked and only have one or two in just a few countries across the world now.

In time, we decided to move to Byron Bay because it was a really like-minded community that was very supportive of what we were doing. Carl came on full-time and we started slowly growing our team. My brother, Manuel joined the company about three years ago. Previously I was doing all the production myself and travelling back to Argentina three times a year - it was getting too intense and we were falling behind on deadlines. He wanted a career change and he's really good with economics and finances, so now he has an office in Argentina with a small team who manages the production, quality control and the weavers' association there. He also comes out to Australia each year. We currently have nine staff with a mix of full and part-time here and in South America. I thought Pampa was going to be much smaller and a nice reflection of Carl and I, but it grew quite quickly and now we're asking ourselves how big and far do we want to grow. Opportunities are endless, but we need to be mindful of what's best for us personally and the people we're working with in South America.

Are there any standout hardships you've come across?

Carl: Our main difficulty, which is also the beauty of Pampa, is working with people so remotely. Many of them are more or less off the grid - they don't have things like the internet. This can make communication really difficult and means we can't just place an order with them like you might a factory. When working between an interior designer in New York who's super busy with strict deadlines and a weaver in remote Latin America, it can get quite tricky.

I had to find something that connected me to my roots and my home.

What have been some key learning experiences?

Carl: Vicky and I went into this with no business experience, so we've really taken baby steps each time we move forward. We try to be really cautious and mindful of each decision and not get swept up in the excitement or demand. We try to stay really grounded.

Pampa is an embodiment of slow age-old artisan production, so we need to be careful of how big we're growing and not lose sight of our roots. Finding that balance can sometimes be difficult with the demand we experience from customers, but it's helpful to keep coming back to those ideals time and time again and base our decisions around them.

How has Pampa positively affected local communities in South America?

Carl: We currently work with 100 to 130 weavers and artisans, all of which are 100 percent Argentinean in mainly northern and central regions. Over time, we've become like extended family with our artisans, which comes from a place of mutual respect.

A lot of the old artisan methods had been lost over the years. Many people had stopped weaving because there was no demand, but now, they're fixing their old looms and teaching their children these ancient practices that can live on. There's a lot of cultural pride in that. But I guess the most obvious way is the financial gain. A lot of our weavers are women, so there's become a sense of pride and community within these women who can now provide for their

families. It's also meant, for some families, that the husband no longer has to travel away for work for months at a time. The whole family can work from home. We're always thinking of how we can continue to give back and that's an ongoing goal for us.

We try to be really cautious and mindful of each decision and not get swept up in the excitement or demand. We try to stay really grounded.

How does your production process differ from other textiles on the market?

Victoria: Our products are 100 percent handmade in every sense of the word. I think that word, *handmade*, is thrown around quite lightly. But our products literally start with the artisan looking for sheep to collect the wool. Yarn is typically spun on a machine and then hand-loomed, but our yarn is hand-spun first and then loomed. A rug might take four weeks (depending on size) and a cushion can take two days just to weave. Our products are also hand-dyed with colours collected from their natural surroundings like tree bark, plants, seeds and rocks.

These elements mean we have a sort of inconsistency within our products. There can be imperfections based on the person who's made it, how long they left it in the dye or which season they were working in. We love this element though; it gives each product a real sense of authenticity and character. It also shows nothing is done by machine, which sets it apart from other textiles.

What, in your eyes, is the company's biggest success?

Victoria: Perseverance. We never thought it would've grown like it has. It started as such a personal thing that was so close to our hearts, we had no idea it would resonate with so many other people.

What does a better world mean to you?

Victoria: Equality. We're lucky to live somewhere

like Australia. Where I'm from, there's a lot of economic and political crisis, a lot of poverty and corruption. So, as a South American girl looking in, Australia is a very privileged country with great opportunities. If more of the world were to have the same equality and security, it would be a better place.

Carl: Less wastefulness, across many avenues.

What would be your biggest sacrifice in running Pampa?

Victoria: Time, definitely. Finding the balance between work and life is really difficult.

Who's your biggest inspiration?

Victoria: My family. My parents have given me a lot and been very supportive.

Carl: One of my best friends, Andre. He has a great work life balance in a successful career and is always my go-to for solid advice.

What does success mean to you?

Victoria: Doing what you love every day.

In the world of environmental sustainability, what's an innovative company you'd recommend and why?

Victoria: TOMS. They give back so much and really take a stand for something positive. And of course Patagonia, being an example of sustainability in the product base industry.

Where do you hope to be five years from now?

Victoria: Continuing to build Pampa, but hopefully with some more spare time, more time to travel and more time for family.

A lot of the old artisan methods had been lost over the years. Many people had stopped weaving because there was no demand, but now, they're fixing their old looms and teaching their children these ancient practices that can live on. There's a lot of cultural pride in that.

GOODFOR
PLASTIC FREE GROCER

JAMES DENTON

AUCKLAND

How did GoodFor come to be?

I was living in Queenstown working at a taco joint that some friends and I started. I guess I've always been a pretty spiritual dude with a love for the outdoors, but it was during this time that I was influenced by some friends to start thinking about my impact and footprint. Once you start concentrating on something, everything starts to waterfall and it's hard to stop noticing. It really started weighing on me.

The taco place naturally ran its course, so my partner Georgie and I moved up to Auckland with her business at the time, which was wellness focused but not really environmentally sustainably focused, so we set about trying to find a way to change that. In the end, we decided to sell it so we could fully immerse ourselves in these newfound values. I personally wanted to find an avenue that I could really sink my teeth in to for the better part of my working career, that would fit in with my personal values. It was actually the first time I'd noticed plastic and the problem it was having on such a grand scale. From there, the idea of GoodFor was born.

I'm also really into design and aesthetics and wanted to create a strong, beautiful brand with a positive message and offering. These are the elements that played into the business for me.

How has the company grown?

Once I had the idea, I did a bunch of market research here and in Australia and then just started driving around Auckland looking for a lease. I was really lucky that our amazing shop space in Ponsonby became available and we managed to get that site before it went to market. It's been three years and we now have six stores, four across Auckland, one in Christchurch and one in Wellington and a large online presence nationwide.

Are there any standout hardships you've come across?

The hardest thing for us has been finding the right lease in the right location. We've developed our business model; we have a good thing going and know exactly where we want to take it but finding the right space to lease has really slowed our growth. We built up our head office and put systems in place based on our business plan for the first five years, now we need to grow our shop locations to utilise it properly. It can be really frustrating to have your vision interrupted by something you didn't foresee and have little control over, not to mention emotionally exhausting.

> It can be really frustrating to have your vision interrupted by something you didn't foresee and have little control over.

What have been some key learning experiences?

I studied finance and accounting in Dunedin. I'm a terrible accountant, but that understanding surrounding business has definitely given me a leg-up.

In that regard, I think respecting money within your company is really important. No matter how much money you make, you should always treat your company as a startup and be really mindful of where each cent is going. Becoming relaxed with money can be a slippery slope. There's also a lot to be said for slow growth. You're better to have one good store than four average ones. In any business decision, stretching yourself too thin can be detrimental and growing organically based on customer demand is really smart. You should never force growth.

How would you best summarise your offering?

We're a beautiful, plastic-free bulk bin store. The idea is that you create zero waste when shopping with us - we've set it up to make it as easy as possible for someone to come and use our services. We wanted to create an environment that serves the customer and the environment equally.

Can you explain the significance of Trees for the Future (trees.org) and what relationship you have with them?

They're an American-based not-for-profit that's been around for roughly twenty-six years. They help communities in Central, East and West Africa by using funds from companies like ours to provide equipment and education that helps communities yield better, stronger crops, plant new crops and grow food forests that thrive in their ecosystem. This organisation works to support the environment, the local people and their social system and educate from a nutritional perspective, so it's really circular. We donate a portion of every sale in store to the foundation, and what's cool is that it's so transparent and accountable. We know the impact we're having and can track it. We've planted over 140,000 trees so far, which means 140,000 customer transactions.

How do your methods at GoodFor aid environmental sustainability?

We're predominantly organic and we work really hard to ensure the back end of the company is zero waste. We try to have a circular economy in place with our suppliers and source from within New Zealand wherever possible, which is often at an extra expense to us. Sourcing locally and supporting the little guy is a really important education piece.

It's common for people to associate organic eating with classism - what do you say to that?

I know a lot of the people who shop with us are making conscious decisions to prioritise eating right and lessening their footprint. These people don't necessarily have lots of money, I think it's just a decision and about where your priorities lie. People will buy a coffee every day or go out for drinks every Friday night, but don't think they have enough money to eat organically.

What does a better world mean to you?

A better world is when people start focusing on things outside of themselves. We can be so self-obsessed and selfish as humans. At the moment we seem to be 'me first, money first' and things like the environment come second, if that. Our impact on the environment isn't a tangible thing to a lot of people, and that's a really big problem.

What effects would you say running a sustainable business has on your immediate community?

I think you can make a huge impact. For us, we've seen it in our customer base and our own neighborhood, by giving people a different option and offering that awareness and education. But also, through other businesses around us who are making small changes to stay competitive or because they've been inspired to become more ethical. We're inundated with emails from people wanting to embark on a similar venture from all over the world, asking for business advice. The butterfly effect is really powerful.

> I think respecting money within your company is really important. No matter how much money you make, you should always treat your company as a startup and be really mindful of where each cent is going.

What, to you, is the company's biggest success?

I look at where we are now and I'm so proud of our team and the way we've evolved. I think our team is really positively impacted from their work environment, which is a pretty cool thing to be putting out into the world.

What would be your biggest sacrifice in running GoodFor?

I would say time, health, friendships and family. I'm so focused and passionate about this, so inevitably I pour so much of myself into it. It can be really emotionally draining at times and I have to be careful about keeping a healthy mental stance and not becoming too consumed by it. Small business is really hard, you kind of get six months where you're just grinding and then you get a big win and are reminded of why you're doing it, but then it's back to the grind again. I've found personally (and from speaking to other business owners, know they feel the same), that it never really stops - the stresses and teething issues. You just get better at dealing with it.

How does environmental sustainability spill into your personal life?

It really flows through everything that I do now. I started small by looking at my plastic consumption, not even that long ago, and it's really spiralled into everything that we do as a family. You start with one glass jar in your pantry and that turns into a whole pantry full of jars, then you move onto your fridge, then you get a worm farm, then another one, and then you get a compost for the stuff the worms can't have, then you're growing vegetables because you want to use your compost. Before you know it, you're pulling apart your bathroom and getting an electric car.

mind, they've just had such a huge impact and are really putting all of their profit back into helping the environment. Locally, companies like Innocent Packaging are taking something that will always be part of our everyday lives and giving the consumer a better option, which is really cool.

Where do you hope to be five years from now?

I hope I'm still running GoodFor and it's grown to where we want it to be. It would be great if I was a little more removed from it by then and have more time for my kids and growing vegetables, surfing, slowing down and taking some time out.

Our impact on the environment isn't a tangible thing to a lot of people, and that's a really big problem.

What are your biggest passions beyond GoodFor?

I love surfing and playing golf. If we lived in a perfect world, I'd love to live close to the beach on a self-sustainable lifestyle block, and surf, play golf and grow vegetables all day.

Who's your biggest inspiration?

I'm a big fan of entrepreneurial giants like Howard Schultz and Steve Jobs. Imagine what could be achieved if you had people like that focusing on something like environmental sustainability? People like that, and Elon Musk, are pretty admirable. They got through so much to be where they are, and it really changed the world.

What does success mean to you?

To create something that I'm really proud of that fits within my values and serves the planet, that can then grow beyond me.

In the world of environmental sustainability, what's an innovative company you'd recommend?

I guess the likes of Patagonia and Tesla come to

Sourcing locally and supporting the little guy is a really important education piece.

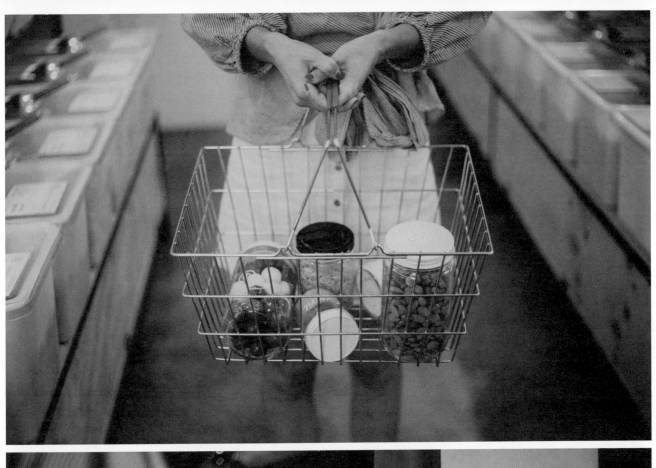

YIN YOGA MATS
YOGA MATS

KIRSTY JAMES

SOUTH GOLDEN BEACH

How did Yin Yoga Mats come to be?

I come from a fashion background and have worked with a few popular fashion labels which meant I saw first-hand the bulk amount of stock and styles that were coming through the country, and the often-undesirable methods they were being shipped in, which I found pretty unsettling.

Yoga was a big part of my life and I'd done my teacher training - that combined with my fashion background and love for design really initiated the brand. The mats felt like the perfect catalyst to combine my work experience and passions.

Once I had the idea and foundations set, I really threw myself into it and went full-time on it from day one. We've now been running for just over two years and have fifteen different designs. I endeavour to keep the collections small and design prints that won't trend as quickly, to instill longevity in the product.

Are there any standout hardships you've come across?

I find transparency within the factories can be quite difficult, especially starting out. When you want to do something that's against the grain, in this case environmentally sustainable and without fabrications and plastics, it's really hard to figure it all out and find a good source in the beginning.

What have been some key learning experiences?

You learn new things every day. There are so many different elements to running a small business, whether it's the creative aspects like design and marketing, doing your accounts or liaising with manufacturers, your focus is always shifting. It can be quite fun having that range in your work, but it definitely takes some time management and discipline, too.

Where can we find your products?

I sell my mats via my own website and wholesale through The Iconic, along with about thirty other stockists predominately in New Zealand and Australia but some as far flung as Switzerland. They're all at similar-minded stores; within yoga studios or at boutique homeware stores.

What's the difference between your production process and that of standard yoga mats on the market?

A lot of yoga mats are made from PVC which is a really harmful plastic that never really biodegrades. The base of our mats is a natural rubber, which is fully biodegradable and is tapped from a tree plantation in Sri Lanka from fully matured trees, so it's a more sustainable option. The top of our mats is made from micro-fibre which is woven by heat and then bonded together. This means both the production process and the end life cycle of the mat is much less harmful to the environment. We're also really mindful of our packaging and shipping methods from the factory to the wholesaler or customer.

What's the best piece of advice you've been given in regard to small business?

Stay true to what you're doing and don't compare yourself to what others are doing around you. Just stay focused on your brand and remember its core values.

And what advice would you give someone?

Just go for it - it can be really fun and exciting. You're creating a life for yourself that's on your own terms rather than working the nine to five life for someone else. It can be really rewarding. But yeah, focus and research are really important aspects that you want to pay attention to. Especially if you're manufacturing something - you should know what it's made from, how it's made, where all the fibres come from and what impact they have. Trace it back to the beginning.

What, in your words, is the importance of community?

Yoga in general has such a huge and embracing community. Before I started yoga, I didn't feel like I had that sense of community with like-minded people. It's a really loving, supportive and empowering space that's largely about taking your practice off the mat and into the world with compassion and mindfulness.

What are your biggest passions beyond Yin Yoga Mats?

We're renovating our house at the moment and I'm loving that process. I guess it comes

back to that design element. It would be quite cool to do some interior design work full-time. My husband is a landscaper and works a lot with design as well, which I love.

Stay true to what you're doing and don't compare yourself to what others are doing around you.

What, to you, is the company's biggest success?

I feel like we're a little too young to have huge success, but I guess all of the beautiful stockists we have is something I'm proud of and thankful for.

What does a better world mean to you?

A world without plastic would be a much better world.

Who's your biggest inspiration?

My husband. He's super talented and creative. He definitely inspires me every day.

Do you live by any mantra?

My daily mantra at the moment is to slow down. It's really hard with a small business to switch off and stop, it becomes such a huge part of your life that it's second nature. So, taking things a bit slower is a conscious effort that's really important for me.

Do you have any daily rituals?

Doing yoga, of course. I also like to burn Palo Santo daily to cleanse my space in the morning, and since we've moved up here from the city, I've been in the ocean every day which has been amazing. It feels so cleansing and is a good way to start your day.

Do you meditate, and if so, in what form?

In poor form - I feel like I go through stages that kind of ebb and flow. I'll get really committed for a while and then fall off track again.

What does success mean to you?

Happiness. Feeling happy, being inspired.

In the world of environmental sustainability, what's an innovative company you'd recommend?

Intimates by the label HARA. I love what they do, their stuff is really beautiful - it's all organic and made from bamboo. They're really focused on making a change environmentally but also by empowering body confidence and women in general. They have a really important message and portray it through beautiful products.

Where do you hope to be five years from now?

Just doing what I'm doing. Doing yoga, hopefully with a nice little studio space.

SUPERNATURAL CELLARS
WINE BAR

PETER WINDRIM

BYRON BAY

How did Supernatural Cellars come to be?

I worked as a biodynamic winemaker and vineyard manager for five years. In this work I learnt a lot about sympathetic agriculture and farming with feeling. I also learnt about instinct and intuition – and how to use your body as an instrument within that. Although obviously beautiful, over time I found that farming can be really isolating and knew it was time for me to move on to a new project. I'd go out to these wine shows and meet great like-minded people with a thirst to learn, but then we'd all separate and go back to our own vineyards. I decided I wanted to bridge that gap by creating a community wine bar that championed the poets of the vines; those growers that are doing the amazing work the right way – where there's zero chemicals, it's organic and biodynamic.

I opened the bar in Byron as I felt as though it was missing that passive education into natural wine. Wine can be really prohibitive and intimidating for a lot of people, so I do a lot by the glass and work around that education to share what I've learnt.

> I wanted to create a feeling of somewhere you may have been in your travels, this reminiscent feeling you can't quite put your finger on. To me, this feels like beautiful parts of Istanbul or Tel Aviv, places from my own travels that I can share.

How would you best summarise your offering?

Essentially, it's about natural wine and salty sea snacks. But on a deeper level, I wanted to create a feeling of somewhere you may have been in your travels, this reminiscent feeling you can't quite put your finger on. To me, this feels like beautiful parts of Istanbul or Tel Aviv, places from my own travels that I can share and where people can have a good time and an experience beyond typical cheese boards and wine tasting. We have fifty winemakers from around the world on our menu, from Margaret River to Austria to Georgia.

> It really derailed that very Western perpetual sense of attainment and achievement; I was working for a big company, making good money, buying the nice things and so forth, but was totally stressed out and hating doing this soul-destroying work.

What led you to biodynamic farming?

Mum and Dad started Krinklewood Vineyard in Hunter Valley about forty years ago, initially going organic and then biodynamic fifteen years ago. I grew up understanding the basics of what was involved. I'd been living in India with my wife working when biodynamics really called me back home.

What were you doing in India?

I was working in Sydney in advertising when my wife Nina had wanted a change of direction, and so we wound up moving to India and I took a job working as the Creative Director for GQ India in Bombay. I was hesitant to take the role initially and move again, having lived abroad several times. I thought I was settled back home in Australia, but it ended up being exactly what I needed. It really derailed that very Western perpetual sense of attainment and achievement; I was working for a big company,

making good money, buying the nice things and so forth, but was totally stressed out and hating doing this soul-destroying work. The job in India of course paid nothing in comparison, but it was so freeing to shed those Western practices and just do something for the love of it. India is an incredibly beautiful, chaotic place. We were living in Bombay in this little village on the waterside - it was so loud and colourful. Everyone there just adopts you with open arms, their humanity blows you away.

We were there for a year before we flew home when my mum was diagnosed with terminal cancer, then I went straight to the farm to be with her and to help Dad. I knew the basics of biodynamics but spent that year reading about fifty books to further my knowledge. It was the philosophies that really got me - the homeopathic application of everything, rather than the science.

We work by rising at dawn and settling at dusk, like the earth and the animals around us.

How would you explain biodynamic farming methods?

I like to think of it as one biological ball of energy. We have cattle, pigs, geese, sheep, chooks and peacocks and they all play an important part. As soon as you remove one of those factors, you notice the shift in the entire dynamic. It teaches you to think about the greater ecosystem as a whole.

A simple example is that because we have a menagerie of native birds, we never have problems with smaller birds eating the grapes. Our pigs are great when you need to loosen up the soil as they roughen it up with their hooves, so instead of having to plough it, they do the job for you. The cattle are also important for their manure which we use to make a tonic that you spray onto the ground in the evening on a descending moon phase. It's a lot about timing. We work by rising at dawn and settling at dusk, like the earth and the animals around us.

How does it differ within the winery?

We remove additions from wine like artificial yeast or sulphur. Fermentation is obviously a critical part of winemaking, so we learn how to achieve this naturally, for example getting your grapes into the winery at the right time of the ascending phase of moon and using that levity (because at this time, liquids and solids are going to rise). If you're doing it during a gravitational phase instead, everything's going to sink to the bottom and it's going to be really difficult to get fermentation happening.

I've never really cared about money, I've had a range of jobs, some paying really nicely, some paying really poorly, but it's never been at my forefront or been my biggest concern. To make a business economically sustainable, however, and be able to keep your doors open, it's something you really have to play into.

It's the same with cutting out fining agents commonly used like fish bladders, skim milk and egg whites (which are the good ones, there are some really bad ones). You want to work with the gravity phase so everything's stuck at the bottom of the tank and you're pumping out the cleaner, clearer liquid from the top.

How would you classify natural wine?

Natural wine, to me, is organic farming by default. Because we don't use any additions on the vineyard or in the winery, most of the wines are un-fined and unfiltered. You end up with the energy, personality and feel of the winemaker which makes it really beautiful and variant each time. Some large conventional wine companies have made it all about science and it's become a textbook formula - the soul, intuition and passion has often been stripped of it.

Have there been any hardships or key learning experiences?

Something from the start that I stuck by was not to compromise, but to share and collaborate, whilst sticking to my vision. Another thing is to really trust in partnership in business, you need to invest in it and treat it like a marriage in its own right.

Something that was new to me though was having to think about the financial side and ensuring its success. I've never really cared about money, I've had a range of jobs, some paying really nicely, some paying really poorly, but it's never been at my forefront or been my biggest concern. To make a business economically sustainable, however, and be able to keep your doors open, it's something you really have to play into. It's a new experience to have to consider that side of things.

How does Supernatural aid environmental sustainability?

We used all recycled materials to fit-out the space and all the food is sourced as locally as possible. We're really big on community and supporting small business, from our ceramics to the staff uniforms and a local painter who did our bar mural. But mostly it's about supporting the winemakers. Being able to support fifty farms around the world and what they stand for is pretty cool.

What's the best piece of advice you've been given in regard to small business?

To back yourself. Trust yourself and your idea and what you have to offer. People will feel it if something is genuine, so if you put your soul into something, people will notice. You just have to put yourself on the line and run the risk.

What, in your words, is the importance of community?

It's a huge one for me. I picked Byron because I knew the community here was really strong with lots of creatives and startups, lots of people in the same boat. That really breeds a culture of people being aware and championing each other. Out on the farm I felt I was missing that sense of community, so it's something that was taken into consideration. Within this space

though I wanted to create a little community surrounding the wine bar with our suppliers, and in the experience and education we offer.

What are your biggest passions beyond this?

Music, surfing, art, photography, friendships and camaraderie. I really learnt that it's important, especially as a man, to foster friendships and be mindful of that.

What does a better world mean to you?

I think travel is important. It teaches you so much empathy, compassion and broad-mindedness. The more you see and experience, the greater the perception and understanding you have within everything else - all the little things of daily life are seen more clearly, and with more gratitude and openness. So, a better world to me is more people seeing life and seeing the world, more independence and freedom rather than getting stuck in a bubble.

Do right by people. Share what you've got and be an unashamedly open-hearted and good person.

Who's your biggest inspiration?

Nicolas Joly, a winemaker from Loire in France. He does terrestrial acupuncture around his vineyard, listening to the earth and realigning accordingly. I was super inspired by him when I started looking into biodynamics.

Do you live by any mantra?

Do right by people. Share what you've got and be an unashamedly open-hearted and good person.

Do you have any daily rituals?

At four o'clock before service every day, no matter what's going on, what mood I'm in or what the weather is doing, I'll go for a swim in the surf. I dive under and have a moment of gratitude. Remaining in check and being aware and thankful is a really good practice. Here at the bar, to start the day I put some flowers and grapes in our vase outside and light some incense as a sort of offering to the wine gods.

What does success mean to you?

Happiness and doing what you love. We only have one life; it goes so fast. Happiness has to be now. It can't be something you save for. Think about what it is that makes you happy - it can, and often will, be simple pleasures. You need to find it and sit with it as often as you can.

In the world of environmental sustainability, what's an innovative company you'd recommend?

I recently met this potter on the Sunshine Coast – his business is called Pān Pottery. This guy makes his own clay, he built his own kiln, he chops his own wood to fire it, he spins everything by hand, and if something uses power, it's solar. Everything in his house he learnt to make himself, from the sink to the table. He's this hugely humble, lovely, happy guy. He burns for it; he bleeds for it. Anything that authentic is just incredible and so inspiring.

Where do you hope to be five years from now?

India? No, but seriously, as a business my passion for this field runs far deeper than this wine bar alone. Personally, I'm very project based. I want to live a life full of projects rather than a life full of endless toil. I don't want to toil away at one thing, ever. So, in five years, who knows, something I love. It's so dangerous to be defined by what you do. Be defined by who you are.

Happiness has to be now. It can't be something you save for.

WHOLE BEINGS
HOLISTIC EDUCATION

NATALIE NELSON + ELYSIA KEILLAH

BURLEIGH, GOLD COAST

How did Whole Beings come to be?

Elysia: We're sisters who'd each worked in early childhood settings for fourteen years after university and felt like we couldn't see ourselves doing it for another ten years. We didn't agree with a lot of the standard teaching curriculum and wanted to find a better way. We wanted a space that taught children on a more holistic level and helped to support mothers, too. We've been running Whole Beings for three years and it's evolved largely into an online platform, which has allowed us to widen our reach.

How has the company grown?

Elysia: We started with small tutoring groups which helped to create a really nice community around us. We decided against registering with the public education system because of all of the red tape and restrictions that would inflict our offering. Now we only have one day each week of classes with the kids locally, which is a really nice way to continue to be hands-on. Internationally, we have roughly 450 monthly subscriptions to our courses across South America, Sweden, England, America, Canada, New Zealand and Australia.

How would you explain Whole Beings' offering?

Elysia: We're a holistic education movement that offers online curriculums for parents to do at home with their children, incorporating mind, body, spirit and community workshop classes. Our programmes currently start at three and go up to six. It's basically a new way of looking at education, based off a standard Australian curriculum. Except we have a lot more freedom with time and exploration of the outdoors, so we can become really creative and personalised, rather than everything being based on templates. We like to focus on real world learning rather than what a classroom with thirty kids and all of the health and safety requirements often restrict you to.

Are there any standout hardships you've come across?

Elysia: We've found there have been a lot of stereotypes to overcome along the way. It's changed a lot in the past three years but homeschooling still has a really old school, negative stigma attached to it. I think in a lot of ways, any time you do something different or put yourself out there creatively, people feel like they have to give their opinion.

We're not the same people we were three years ago, put it that way. There have been countless times when we've thought, oh it would be so much easier to just go get a job back in teaching, what are we doing? But getting through those tough moments is really what makes you stronger and forces you to thrive in what you're doing. I would say there are challenges every day, but it's how you handle them that decides the outcome and your fate. It's about showing up again and again, despite the difficulties, that gets you through.

> ## We're not the same people we were three years ago, put it that way.

What have been some key learning experiences?

Natalie: For us it's learning how to remove the fear. Each decision can be scary and feel like a risk, but when you remove all the pressure and fear, you can really grow and prosper.

How is your offering different to other schooling programmes?

Natalie: I think it largely comes down to the red tape within government and the pressure that's on teachers and schools to get through so much with one teacher to a whole classroom - it can become about ticking all the boxes and nothing more. For example, we don't like to separate topics; it's not literacy, now math, now art or science. It's like "*let's go outside and look at bees and their hives, let's talk about how their bodies work, what they create, how they impact the world, how they sound, where you can find them... and then start looking into their honey and see what's interesting about that, can we bake with it? How can we implement science and math into baking?*"

Elysia: We take everyday interactions and turn them into real learning experiences that leave the child filled with creativity, curiosity, awareness and empathy for the world around them. It inspires them to look at the world that way all the time, rather than separating school time and play time.

There's also a lot of pressure for children to learn the same way. Many children might struggle in a school setting where it's largely book work, but thrive using their hands or being active or in art. But in a school setting they often get left behind in their studies, and it results in them playing up because they feel like they're not smart enough or that they don't fit in or understand. This kind of labelling can really dictate their entire schooling life.

When any of us feel we're not good at something, we lose self-confidence and steer away from it, naturally. In a classroom setting it can be difficult for teachers to detect things like this with individuals or have time to do a lot about it. It can easily become a really negative perpetual cycle.

It's about showing up again and again, despite the difficulties...

How does your offering aid environmental sustainability?

Natalie: All of our programmes have an environmental element, whether it's learning about how to respect the land, sea or animals, or thrifting, reusing materials or growing vegetables. We also don't use plastic in any of our curriculums. Even if you're not directly saying things to the kids, you're leading by example and normalising certain habits. Talking about how we can make our own paper and why that's better, and then being mindful of how much we throw in the bin or what we can reuse in other crafts, goes a long way.

What, in your words, is the importance of community?

Elysia: Community is everything - if you don't have it, life's a pretty lonely journey. We've found people are always seeking a community and sense of belonging and support.

What, in your eyes, is the company's biggest success?

Natalie: I think showing up for three years with such a new concept and really giving it our all. It doesn't surprise me that many companies shut down after a year. It's so hard and takes so much of yourself and so much sacrifice to run a small business or startup. We're really proud of sticking at it and how far we've come.

What does a better world mean to you?

Elysia: Everyone acknowledging that we're all connected and one and the same. Division is just ego.

Natalie: If people could have real values and real foundations like compassion and empathy and mindfulness, we'd all benefit.

Success is such a strange concept. It's so varied and personal and yet we all try to be the version that society tells us to be, which is actually impossible.

Who's your biggest inspiration?

Elysia: We're really inspired by Brené Brown. I think her take on shame is really powerful, especially when applied to the schooling system. Methods like star charts and shaming children into success might work in the short term of a spelling test but it also manifests into so many internal issues within kids such as anxiety, fear and self-doubt.

Natalie: Joe Dispenza; he's changed my life, the person I am and how I operate in the world.

Do you have any daily rituals?

Natalie: We do Joe Dispenza meditations and make time for a walk or daily coffee. Being mindful to enjoy those little pleasures in life and really making time for them are non-negotiables which can be really important when you're self-employed.

What does success mean to you?

Elysia: Success is such a strange concept. It's so varied and personal and yet we all try to be the version that society tells us to be, which is actually impossible.

Natalie: I think it's being happy and having balance. But there's never an end result for happiness or success. It's about the journey and being present every day to find those things.

In the world of environmental sustainability, what's an innovative company you'd recommend?

Elysia: I'd say The Farm in Byron Bay is doing some incredible things. Their collective and community is amazing. They really are educating every single person who walks in there and creating change in so many avenues.

Where do you hope to be five years from now?

Elysia: We hope that there can be more Whole Beings hubs and little community groups like this around the world with these values that act as a place of support. We'd also love to be able to create a mindfulness programme that schools can take on and implement properly, too.

Everyone acknowledging that we're all connected and one and the same. Division is just ego.

FORAGE + BLOOM
BOTANICAL TEAS

HANNAH MCMENAMIN

AUCKLAND

How did Forage + Bloom come to be?

While I was working as a barista at a friend's café in Melbourne, I became really fascinated with the different ways you could extract coffee and the different effects these methods had on the body. I'd worked largely in hospitality over the years whilst travelling and was already a coffee geek, but it was here I started really learning about the chemistry, constituents and flavour profiles of the plant itself, depending on how you used it. This interest ultimately led me to study naturopathy, nutrition and herbal medicine back in New Zealand. During my studies, I became really passionate about bringing those medicinal qualities into our everyday lives in a way that tasted good and was accessible. I wanted to challenge the perception that herbal medicine had to taste unpleasant for it to work.

After I graduated in 2012 I lived in Rome for a year. I didn't work in the industry there but wanted to make sure I was staying connected to the herbal world. I ended up finding this tiny little dispensary from the 1500s that'd been passed down through family lineage. It was musty and every wall was lined with drawers filled with herbs. I met the owner, Paolo, and we totally vibed off each other – it turned out he was one of the top dogs in herbal medicine in Rome. I ended up spending quite a lot of time there, speaking with him and observing how he practised. He worked with dried herbs more than fluid extracts, which was different to how we practised in New Zealand. I'd grown medicinal herbs during my studies and loved the idea of using this gentle remedy in a therapeutic setting. This concept grew into Forage + Bloom.

How has the company grown?

When I arrived back in New Zealand, I was talking about my idea with friends over dinner one evening. They happened to be involved in a new café opening and asked me to blend my teas for them. Because of my background in hospitality, I

thought that creating a range of herbal teas to fit into the café/bar/restaurant scene would be a great way to share the health benefits of herbs in an everyday setting. I designed the range around your typical well-known tea flavours, but with a therapeutic twist. The idea became a reality, the teas were a hit, and it's been all go since then.

My company has grown really organically over its five-year lifespan. I worked full time managing Tonic Room (a herbal dispensary) for the first three years until Forage + Bloom grew into my full-time gig. I've been really lucky to work alongside many health-conscious and sustainably minded establishments and the demand for what I do only continues to grow, which is an awesome sign of the times.

What's the difference between your products and regular teas on the market?

Sustainability of medicinal plants is a big interest of mine, so all the herbs I use grow in abundance and have no chance of becoming endangered. Organically grown is a must, and there are never any additives or flavourings, just good old-fashioned herbs.

> ## I realised that I'd been treating my business like it was my boss, instead of making it work for me.

Are there any standout hardships you've come across?

There are constantly a million things you could or should be doing in small business, and my mentality was always to push through and get it done. I eventually experienced a pretty massive burnout and started suffering from huge anxiety attacks, which was really out of character for me. I was working sixty-hour weeks for years on end – it was just too much.

It was all a big wakeup call and a reminder that I needed to slow down and look after my own health going forward.

What have been some key learning experiences?

I think self-care can be lost within small business.

I think self-care can be lost within small business. My whole business was based on helping others to be healthy, and yet I wasn't showing myself the same care.

HANNAH MCMENAMIN — FORAGE + BLOOM

My whole business was based on helping others to be healthy, and yet I wasn't showing myself the same care. Finding that time for myself was key. I realised that I'd been treating my business like it was my boss, instead of making it work for me. Learning to say "no thank you" was a huge part of that and a really big lesson.

How does the production of Forage + Bloom aid environmental sustainability?

Medicinal herb sustainability is very important to me. This is why I use herbs that grow in abundance and in many cases are classed as weeds. My packaging is biodegradable, recyclable and compostable. I believe that I have a responsibility to be environmentally ethical in my business practices.

What would be your biggest sacrifice in running a small business?

Going through a period of severe anxiety. I'd never felt that before, and it hit hard. Although it was a tough time, it did teach me a lot about how to look after myself.

How does environmental sustainability spill into your personal life?

It's really important to me. I do what I can, and I choose to support businesses and practices that are environmentally conscious. I'm quite an essentialist – I'd rather consume less, and of higher quality. I'm mostly plant-based, I shop at the farmers' market, I like to buy ethically made clothing from local companies, I grow a garden and have a worm farm, that kind of thing. I mean, I'm no angel – I enjoy a nice cocktail and drive a car – but I feel best when I'm living a simple, low-impact and thoughtful life, and am close to nature. I'm really grateful for what this planet offers us, and I try not to take that for granted.

What's your go-to when you're in a creative rut?

I'm super creative so rarely find myself in a rut, but if I'm struggling, I always find getting out of my mind and into my body is a quick fix to change my state. A walk or run in nature is a go-to for sure.

Who's your biggest inspiration?

My greatest mentor, Kate Robertson. Such an incredibly knowledgeable herbalist and so real as a person. I worked alongside her for nine years and learnt so much, particularly in the field of herbal formulating and manufacturing.

Do you live by a mantra?

"People don't change (unless they want to). Humans are unique in their ability to willingly change. We can change our attitude, our appearance and our skillset. But only when we want to. The hard part, then, isn't the changing it. It's the wanting it." – Seth Godin.

What does success mean to you?

Ultimately feeling happy and contributing my creativity and expertise to help others.

In the world of environmental sustainability, what's an innovative company you'd recommend and why?

Country Kitchen. Hannah Jack, its founder, champions the organic growth of over 100 medicinal herbs here in New Zealand and uses them in her beautiful skincare products. Her work is so important for plants, people and the planet and is filled with integrity.

Where do you hope to be five years from now?

My passion is formulating and manufacturing herbal extracts of all kinds. I love understanding how herbs work and taste, and how best to extract their qualities for desired actions. Lately I've been working on product formulation for companies that wish to create herbal and botanical products. I see this as being a big part of my future as a herbalist. It's a great way to keep my passion alive and continue using my knowledge for good.

THE FARM BYRON BAY
COLLABORATIVE FARMERS

EMMA +
TOM LANE

How did The Farm come to be?

We were living in Sydney at the time and often spent our weekends taking the children out to Tom's parents' farm so they could get out of the city and reconnect with the land. Eight years ago, just after our fourth child, we decided to buy land in the rolling hinterlands of Byron as we both knew and loved the area - although it was a bit of a learning curve as we didn't know a lot about growing or farming at that point. We had a thirty-acre working farm in Federal with pigs, beef, chicken, goats, lambs and a half-acre of vegetables which supplied us with sixty to seventy percent of our food. We'd fly up from Sydney any chance we could get.

One day, our three-year-old Matilda went missing. We found her down the back of the vegetable garden, sat on the ground, with her t-shirt slung up picking and eating the green beans that she'd grown. It really made us stop and think if we could give that to our own child, that special relationship with the land and her own food, how could we do that on a larger scale? We wanted to do it for everyone - a farm for the people.

It's been running now for five years and going from strength to strength. From day one it's been more successful than we thought it would be. People have been yearning to get back to the land.

What did you set out to achieve?

For a lot of people, it's quite rare to be on a working farm. If you don't have access to land, you can come here, have a picnic, use the space and see how it all works. There's a huge educational opportunity within that.

We created this space and then invited other people to become part of the community. We started by putting a tender out for a restaurant and were inundated with applicants. It's really taken on a life of its own and grown hugely since then.

Our fundamentals, which businesses sign up to, is to grow, feed, educate and give back. To grow this and our surrounding community, to feed the earth and the people, and within that everything has to have an element of education.

We want everyone who leaves here to feel like they've learnt something and that their impact can make a difference, no matter who they are, where they live or what resources they have. And to give back to both the land and community. For example, we've planted over 7,500 trees, created seventy tonnes of organic matter, we support community groups and have a vegetable plot allocated to a local charity that gives food to the homeless and those in need.

Everyone knows their doctor or their dentist, and yet we eat three times a day and most people don't know their farmer. We go to the supermarket and have this huge disconnection - so we're not eating seasonally, locally or intuitively. We wanted to help change that.

> Everyone knows their doctor or their dentist, and yet we eat three times a day and most people don't know their farmer. We go to the supermarket and have this huge disconnection.

The Farm, simply put, provides a space for a microcosm of small businesses within it. Can you explain how it works?

It's like an incubator model and a village where everyone is co-dependent. We have farm rules, a mission statement and set of values that businesses here operate by. We provide the space - be it land or buildings and a degree of equipment, machinery and resources - then act as a support system to get those businesses up and running. It's an invaluable resource for startup companies and young farmers who don't have the financial backing to buy land or want to be small scale because, for a lot of them, there's guaranteed customers on their doorstep.

Everything grown on the land goes through the restaurant, bakery or produce store. The growers then know that their product is already sold to the restaurant and the restaurant knows its ingredients will be picked, washed and brought over as fresh as can be. Everything grown is instantly sold, which makes cash flow and business security much easier.

There are roughly a dozen other micro-businesses on the farm. To name a few, there's a bakery, gelato bar, florist and nursery (who grow and sell on site and offer workshops), an apiary, composting company, botanical garden (which is made into natural organic skincare) and the restaurant. There are four to five independent horticulture growers who have up to an acre each and a meat protein farmer working with eggs, chickens, sheep, pigs and beef.

The ripple effect of this is that although we're collectively growing twenty tonnes of produce per year, we need four times that - so there's another twenty or thirty other local organic farmers that are also benefitting from the demand that this space has created.

It's an old fashioned, new farming model. Really, it's how our grandparents would've grown up with that sense of community, and yet it's new in this day and age because we've become so individualistic about business. This farm community is not just about me and Tom, it's about the community of people who make up the farm.

Are there any standout hardships you've come across?

From the outside, what we do personally looks really simple and popular, so we get a lot of opinions and negative feedback from people who don't understand. We've had to work really hard to get those people to understand our workload, the risks we've taken and our intention - which is to be a support system, not competition.

What have been some key learning experiences?

Being really clear from the get-go on what we were trying to create and how we translated that was really important, especially with so many moving parts and people involved. We wrote our values list on day one and it's important that we all keep coming back to that, so we keep our vision focused.

There's a lot to be said for being able to hand things off to the experts and have a good team around

you. At the beginning, we were here day and night in the office and then going out and planting rows of vegetables. But in time, you realise where you're most valuable to the business. We have a great team around us now for that reason. You also have to be careful to create something that's sustainable for the long term, so putting it before our own growing family or wellbeing means it isn't going to last long. There can be a lot of guilt attached to that, but you have to know your strengths and trust your team and their strengths in order to grow as a business.

Sustainability is important in all avenues, especially economically so that it can prosper and continue to help others.

Can you explain why the 'farm to table' practice is so beneficial?

From its simplest level, it's about knowing where your food comes from, where it's grown, what it's grown with and what chemicals may be attached. So again, it's about educating people.

It can be a little confronting or controversial for some people that we have the pigs in the paddock, and at the same time there might be a pig on the spit in the restaurant courtyard, and we understand that. But we believe that pig is running around in the pasture like it's meant to be - it's not on a concrete pad, in a shed, locked in a pen or chained up. It's not filled with antibiotics. It's fed natural organic produce. Unfortunately, that's not the case for most pork you might come across in a supermarket or on a menu. People might be happy to disconnect and buy if from a supermarket with the meat covered in plastic and not know how it was raised, what it was fed, how it was treated, how long its life was or any of these details, but turning a blind eye isn't helping anyone - not you, not the pig, not the land.

We also believe that if you're going to kill an animal you make use of it, you don't just use that one cut. This is where the guys at the restaurant

are incredible. They come up with interesting ways to use every part of that animal, from the meat to the ears. It's the same with vegetables, they're creative with what they have in their backyard and make sure they're utilising all of it.

What about from an environmental perspective?

The aspect of food miles and nutrition comes into play - not only is it organic and grown in healthy, nutrient-dense soil, but it's so fresh. It doesn't have sprays, it isn't refrigerated to keep it brighter or fresh longer. If you really sit and think about all of the hands and processors that go into getting food to a supermarket, to be stacked on a shelf, sprayed in Sulphur to keep colour before you buy it, take it home and eat it - it's a lot. It's a lot of energy, a lot of travel miles and CO_2 emissions, a lot of chemicals. Here, there's no packaging. No middleman.

So, to us it's about the education, the environmental and health benefits, and respecting the animal and the farmer. When people have an understanding of this workload, they appreciate their food more and waste less.

Before we bought it, this was eighty acres of slightly unproductive land with a few cows on it. Together, we've turned it into a very productive space across so many elements.

What effects would you say running a sustainable business has on your immediate community?

It's beneficial in many ways. It benefits all those families that don't have a place where they can run and be free with their kids. People come here just to walk their dogs and treat it like a park. We have daycare and school groups coming through all the time to use the space, and our charity partnerships also benefit the wider community in lots of different ways.

On a different scale, it's attracting like-minded people to tell their story by using our space. We have people from all over the world coming and running workshops or events to tell their wellness or environmental impact story. We don't need to be the ones beating the drum all the time, we can just supply the space for others to - we've had such a huge voice across the world because of this.

What, in your eyes, is the company's biggest success?

Creating community and connecting people to real food. When we have school groups come through and we see the kids pulling a carrot out from the ground, their little faces lit up in amazement, you realise how disconnected we've become.

I guess it's also about how successful the venture has been. Everyone thought we were crazy selling our house to fund this. The day we opened we were hiding our tears with sunglasses as people poured through the gates; people showing up. For us, that's a huge success. And with that, the sustainability of the project, from an environmental perspective of course but economically, too. We couldn't have done half of what we have or grown in this way (nor continue to grow) if we hadn't set it up and run it properly from a financial perspective. Sustainability is important in all avenues, especially economically so that it can prosper and continue to help others.

What does success mean to you?

Seeing our kids recognise what we're doing and be a part of this crazy journey we're on. That makes us really proud. They recognise the risks we've taken and the benefits of those risks, which we feel is hugely successful.

What would be your biggest sacrifice in running a small business?

From the outside it all looks very dreamy. But it's a lot of hard work, a lot of time, a lot of big decisions to make that affect an entire village and lots of other people's livelihoods. We feel accountable in that regard.

We're also always 'on.' No matter where we are in the world or what we're doing, we're at the beck and call of the business. But that's also such an incredible space to be in with constant creativity and growth, which is really exciting. We have huge plans - this is just the beginning. But we have four kids, and they need to come first, so we need to be careful with our time, too.

I know you've had a couple of other big projects in the works recently - do you want to talk us through those?

Our sister project, The Beach House, is a 2.5-acre venue right on the beach. Launched in November 2019 in East Ballina, it's all about the coastal and marine ecosystem. It's a celebration of conservation, so it has the same principles and values as The Farm but through a different platform. It's a venue with attached accommodation for event hire, and we plan on offering workshops to integrate the environment and sustainability through the facility. We've linked up with three ambassadors - Positive Change for Marine Life, Ballina Coastcare and Australian Seabird Rescue - and have an environmental trust. Every event we have, money goes into this trust which we then use to work with our ambassadors. The idea is that we celebrate life, but let's have consciousness with the planet and our actions, too.

We also completed our house build, The Range in 2018, which was a huge passion project that sits on 120 acres up in the hills. We had it built out of found and foraged building materials. All the stonework is from stones foraged off of the property, the roof is made out of an old bridge that we found, and the shelves on the walls are the old homes' trusses. We collect our own water, do our own sewage and generate eighty percent of our own power, which we hope to make 100 percent soon. We plan on growing all of our own food and want to plant out the land in trees around us to return it to its former rainforest, which works out to roughly 50,000 trees over the next ten years.

In the world of environmental sustainability, what's an innovative company you'd recommend?

There are so many incredible companies out there now, we definitely feel a huge shift happening. We love what B Corp do. They review and grade companies all over the world based on their impact socially and environmentally, which is a great tool for the consumer. Small Giants are amazing, they're buying into companies that aid the community and environment and help them get off the ground. We're talking millions of dollars being poured into a range of different businesses, which is an incredible opportunity to a lot of people looking to make change.

Where do you hope to be five years from now?

We still hope to be in the Byron region. We're obviously really passionate about The Farm, The Beach House and our house, The Range, so we'll be working to continue to grow those platforms. But we hope to see another two or three places like The Farm set up around the world and watch the ripple effect of that education, growing from the little pebble to the biggest stone.

FAIR + SQUARE
SOAP

CARLY LOW

TUTUKAKA COAST

How did Fair + Square come to be?

To be honest, it was by accident. About ten years ago someone gave me a soap-making kit as a present. For around five years I pottered around making soap at home and as gifts because I really enjoyed the methodical process involved in making it and noticed the difference in my own skin. It never occurred to me that it could become a business. It's been amazing, but also quite a shock, that demand has continued to grow. I didn't know anything about starting a business or what that entailed, but it's been a really slow progression that's grown with me, so I've been able to learn each stage as it comes.

How has the company grown?

It really has grown far beyond what I ever planned. We now have 100 stockists across New Zealand and around 30 others waiting on a backlist. Huge department stores have approached us too, but we're still really small scale and want to keep it that way, so we need to find balance in our growth and output.

Are there any standout hardships you've come across?

Due to the relaxed nature and slow growth of the business I was able to avoid a lot of those usual small business pains and pressures. When we had our children, we'd shuffled our family finances so that I could be a stay-at-home mum, which meant when the business started, we didn't have a huge financial strain where I had to be bringing in an income. It wasn't like a lot of other companies where there's a huge initial outlay.

What have been some key learning experiences?

When I first started, I really wanted to do everything myself. As Kiwis, we often have a lot of pride attached to that and a 'do it yourself' mentality where we can keep things quite close. As a woman in business, I think there's this added pressure to feel like you have to prove yourself and that you don't need help. But it actually ends up being really unhealthy for you and the business when you try and do everything.

One thing after another, I slowly started to let go. I learnt to outsource things like packaging, branding and photography and I found it was super empowering to have this amazing team around me. It also gave me time to focus on making the soap and doing what I'm good at. Outsourcing areas that weren't my specialty has meant the business has really flourished.

I'd also definitely recommend being vulnerable and asking for help. I learnt it's about the community around the brand, not just about me.

What's the difference between your products and regular soap on the market?

I work with cold-processed soap. It's a really old, traditional method where you combine an alkali substance called lye with oils or fats at a certain temperature, which causes a chemical reaction called saponification. Once these two substances have been combined at that temperature, there's no trace of either oil or lye present in the compound, so it completely transforms into a new substance that's essentially a salt or soap. It gets poured into moulds and sits for six weeks to cure and then we're left with a hard mass. Another key difference is that I use natural therapeutic grade essential oils, rather then synthetics and cosmetic grade fragrance, and leave the glycerin in so it's really nourishing and moisturising for your skin.

Commercial soap isn't even classified as 'soap' as a compound. It's usually just a detergent combined with chemicals and artificial lathering agents that are formed into a bar. They usually extract the glycerin from the soap because it's a high value ingredient that they can add to things like moisturisers instead with a higher price point. If they were to leave that element in the soap, it wouldn't be profitable for them to sell it for a dollar per bar.

Palm oil is also commonly used within commercial mass-produced soaps and is super destructive for the environment. It's really cheap and is one of the best oils you can use to get a hard soap that lasts a long time and makes a good lather. I use cocoa butter instead, which has really similar properties.

How does environmental sustainability spill into your personal life?

We live pretty self-sustainably out here. A few years ago, I did a course in organic and biodynamic farming so that we could use these methods

As a woman in business, I think there's this added pressure to feel like you have to prove yourself and that you don't need help. But it actually ends up being really unhealthy for you and the business when you try and do everything.

on our own eight-acre lifestyle block. We do things like beneficial planting and composting to help aid the environment, so we don't need to use nasty toxins. We also grow most of our own vegetables organically, have horses and raise our own chickens and beef for meat, eggs and milk.

I'd also definitely recommend being vulnerable and asking for help.

My husband built our tiny home and is really passionate about passive houses that are smart and functional. Our power bill is around $70 per month with a family of four — we've just installed solar panels, which will of course bring it down lots more. So it really does flow through everything that we do.

I believe you should be trying to stay away from harmful chemicals and synthetics any way you can.

How do you find the work life balance with young children?

It definitely is a struggle with the kids. Rye is four and Quincy is three, so neither are at school yet. They go to daycare two days a week and initially I had a lot of guilt attached to that, but once I moved past my own ego I realised it's actually so much better for them to have a few days away from me and off the farm. It also means the two days they're there I can really invest myself into work, and then when they're home, I can give them my all.

What does a better world mean to you?

More simplicity. There's so much choice now and I think we can become a bit bombarded by that. Stripping it back to basics and slowing everything down is really beneficial.

How has running a sustainable business affected your immediate community?

People within our community take it on personally and feel really proud and attached to the brand and products. They feel really included because they've seen it from the ground up, which helps to create so much awareness around the quality and worth of the products.

What, in your eyes, is the company's biggest success?

Probably the conversation it starts and awareness that it brings.

What would be your biggest sacrifice in running a small business?

Time with the children, definitely. I really had this vision of being an all-encompassing mother that was theirs full time, but as life has evolved, this business has become another baby that demands my attention too. I've had to split myself across both, which isn't what I expected and has been a bit of a sacrifice at times.

What does success mean to you?

Being able to support my family and people within our community.

In the world of environmental sustainability, what's an innovative company you'd recommend?

Ethique. I love how focused they are on reducing plastic and the awareness surrounding that.

Where do you hope to be five years from now?

For me, this business serves as something I can be passionate about and a way to contribute positively to society as well as have balance in my own life. Ideally, if both my husband and I could work three days a week, and we're able to employ a few others and give them support and opportunities, that's a pretty ideal balance for me. That's the goal. Progress for progress's sake isn't my game.

I believe you should be trying to stay away from harmful chemicals and synthetics any way you can.

POCKET CITY FARMS
URBAN GROWERS

EMMA BOWEN + MICHAEL ZAGORIDIS

SYDNEY

How did Pocket City Farms come to be?

Emma: We've both always had a pretty strong core interest in sustainability within our personal lives. I was working as an editor for a sustainable living magazine and Zag was working within publishing as well. He'd been getting a little antsy with all the time spent behind a computer screen, wanting to be outdoors and using his hands more. He quit his job to learn how to farm. Around the same time, I interviewed Brooklyn Grange in New York which is a large rooftop farm. We became quite inspired and wanted to do something similar here.

From there, we both sought out farming experience for a few years, as that was relatively new to us, and started talking to landlords and councils. It took about three years before we secured this space. We opened in June 2016 but had access to the site a year before to get the crops started.

> ## I think we've learnt more in the last five years doing this than we did in ten years in other professions.

Michael: After the initial idea, we started to shift our lives towards that direction. We started learning more about permaculture, too, which really resonated with us. On one of our permaculture courses we met our co-founder, Karen Erdos. It was super daunting in the beginning, I remember opening up this book on organic vegetable farming and thinking to myself *"I really don't know anything, I'm literally starting from a blank page"*.

What did you set out to achieve?

Emma: In its simplest form, we didn't know where our food was coming from or have that connection living in the city – it made us wonder how many other people were feeling the same way? It's the simplest way you can get farming in front of people and start them on their own journey of understanding the time and hard work that goes into their food, and the importance of knowing where it comes from.

Are there any standout hardships you've come across?

Michael: There were a lot of times we thought we had a green light and were deep in negotiation and then it fell through, so it was definitely an emotionally exhausting journey to get the space open for business. Finding a space like this in the central city, especially back then when it was such a new idea, was really challenging. We've also had a couple of tough storms to get through, which is of course always going to be a large element of horticulture that's out of our control.

Emma: Another thing that can be a struggle is how dynamic you have to be. Because we have this really varied business across growing, education and being a community space, it can be a bit of a juggle.

What have been some key learning experiences?

Michael: Learning to let go of things out of your control like the weather has been an important one, and to understand that no matter how long you've been doing it, you're always learning.

Emma: I think we've learnt more in the last five years doing this than we did in ten years in other professions.

In what ways has Pocket City Farms created a sense of community?

Michael: That sense of community and education and being able to expose people to what we're doing here has always been a large part of it. Through our volunteer programmes, we've noticed we've created this really strong sense of community and a network of like-minded people of varying ages and backgrounds that have, in many cases, spread much further than us. Those people are of course getting a lot out of the farm (the people who came here to seek education), but we've also noticed that it's affected the people who come here every day, like the mum groups or coffee drinkers - they're

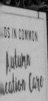

just poking their heads over the fence and noting the changes season to season. The subliminal education of what's going on can be really powerful.

Emma: Along with the educational farming side, we run events like potluck dinners and something called Farm Chats where we pull in a panel of people to talk about different topics. Our most recent one, for example, was about horticulture therapy and the benefits of gardening for mental health. So, we get 100 people come along and get involved in that conversation. We planted a food forest early on that's 180sqm along the footpath full of fruit trees, shrubs, herbs, nuts and other edibles that's free for the community to collect from. More recently, we've started a community compost collection where people can bring their food scraps in. We have Milkwood who run their workshops here, collaborate with Crop Swap Sydney once a month and have loads of school groups come through.

We try to live by community sufficiency, rather than self-sufficiency, in all areas of our lives and believe that's the key to a better world.

How do you find work life balance with a young family?

Emma: I work part time - we had our son Banjo just as we opened the farm (as Murphy's law goes). There was a lot of front-pack wearing going on in those early days, and Michael works full-time as the farm manager.

Who do you supply products to?

Michael: We supply about eight hospitality kitchens regularly and quite a lot of Ooooby's food boxes (we take a lot of their food scraps, too). And then we sell at markets weekly. We've also recently set up a farm-style honesty box here for people to buy produce.

What methods does Pocket City Farms use to aid the environment?

Michael: We farm organically and ecologically, which means we work to boost the biodiversity within the soil to make it really nutrient dense. This style of farming also boosts our organic matter, which helps with things like water retention and requires less watering through summer. We make all of our own compost, which is pretty important, and we've been dabbling in biodynamics. We aim to get some better practices in place to further aid that too, which give back to the land.

What, in your eyes, is the company's biggest success?

Michael: Community building and the way that's taken on a life of its own. On hard days, when we can see that sense of community around us, it really makes it all worth it. And we wouldn't be able to do it without them.

What would be your biggest sacrifice in running Pocket City Farms?

Emma: Self-care, there's been a big lack of that over the past few years.

Michael: That's not an unfamiliar story with small business owners and farmers too, but there's been a few breakages - you really throw your whole self into it, emotionally and physically.

What does a better world mean to you?

Emma: Firstly, one where people are kind to each other, animals and themselves. If you can be really truly kind, everything else will flow from there. I also think there's this mentality where people don't think what they do matters because they're one person but being part of a movement can really change things. We've become so disconnected from things that really matter, from things that bring us real joy.

Michael: A world where everything isn't viewed as a financial commodity. This mentality of things or time only being worth the money you can make from it makes it really hard to slow down and live a simpler, healthier life.

In the world of environmental sustainability, what's an innovative company you'd recommend?

Within our own industry, I'd say Milkwood who run permaculture courses and Ooooby vegetable boxes. We love what those companies offer and the support that they give.

Where do you hope to be five years from now?

Emma: Maybe with another farm or two. We've seen the positive impact this has had on our community and it would be cool to see that happen in different areas.

EMMA BOWEN + MICHAEL ZAGORIDIS — POCKET CITY FARMS

I remember opening up this book on organic vegetable farming and thinking to myself "I really don't know anything, I'm literally starting from a blank page".

LITTLE COMPANY
SKINCARE THERAPIST

STACEY BURT

BYRON BAY

How did Little Company come to be and how has it grown?

I'd worked in the spa industry for fifteen years and noticed the beauty industry was in need of positive change. I was seeing unhappy therapists and unhappy practices, so opening a space was my vehicle to deliver that necessary change.

I initially opened a little boutique with a friend in Hawthorn, Melbourne, which quickly generated a cult following. We soon realised we were extremely over-subscribed, the physical space being small with not much room to grow. In the end, we realised we had different objectives with the business, so we decided to part ways. Little Company was born from there.

Little Company became centred on creating a nourishing experience, not only for our customers but also my team. It's been four years now and we have a space in Byron and in Melbourne, and we're starting the process of introducing our own products.

How would you best summarise your offering?

Little Company is a skin and wellness studio. Founded originally in Melbourne in 2015, we built our foundation on sustainable environmental standards and skincare practices. I believe that beauty isn't made, but cultivated through how we live, what we eat and how we think. This philosophy also goes deeper than just our skincare routines - it's how we live. We work with living ingredients, both in and on the skin.

We also designed our two studios to be places where clients can pause, reset and nourish while giving their skin some love, which is an important element.

Are there any standout hardships you've come across?

Definitely, it was a challenging start! Our daughter Lex was just three weeks old when Little Company first came to life. For some reason, I always open new spaces with newborns. When we moved our family up to Byron Bay, our second daughter, Stevi, was only

ten weeks. Opening in a totally new location with very young children brings many challenges, both personally and professionally - mainly by not being able to dedicate enough time to a new business. We also found the new dynamic and lifestyle in Byron Bay meant we needed to revisit the pillars of our brand and how we reached a different type of customer.

We really immersed ourselves into the community as a form of market research to find the best way to serve this new clientele. The initial incubation and launch of a business is critical to creating momentum and I find that PR efforts are often overlooked within small business, but can be an imperative lifeline, especially early on.

What have been some key learning experiences?

Learning to trust and let go. It's so easy to try and control as it feels familiar and safe, but growth comes with trust.

I believe that beauty isn't made, but cultivated through how we live, what we eat and how we think.

Can you explain the difference between Little Company and regular beauty therapy spaces?

Our 'living skin' philosophy emphasises treating the skin as a living, breathing organ. We use products that feed your skin the nutrients it needs. Ranging in focus from relaxing to correcting, our facials serve as a vital educational step in developing a daily, in-home skincare routine for sustainable, long-term results.

We use only natural, organic, cruelty-free skincare products and incorporate meditation, ancient practices and wisdom into all of our treatments. We also believe that your skin is a reflection of what's happening on the inside; skincare is as much about diet as it is the products you use topically.

To me, beauty and skincare is an ongoing ritual, and a constantly evolving process. Our goal is to educate women on how their skin works and reacts, so that they understand what they can do every day to feel beautiful in the skin they're in.

What, in your words, is the importance of natural skincare?

Natural skincare is more important than ever. We're living in a world where manufacturers are forever finding ways to cut costs with quick fixes, but nature is a more reliable source.

We ensure that each ingredient found inside our range can be traced back to its origin. All our products must be locally sourced, cruelty-free, and entirely plant-based as a rule of thumb.

The initial incubation and launch of a business is critical to creating momentum...

How does Little Company aid environmental sustainability?

The Byron Bay studio was designed with the environment at the forefront of every decision. The studio is built from sustainably-sourced (upcycled and recycled) timber and natural stone, and is powered entirely by ten kilowatt solar energy.

Natural rubber tiles make up the flooring, meanwhile low-VOC paint coats every natural timber surface. To reduce carbon emissions, the studio's furnishings, hardware and decor were sourced within Australia and styled by an Australian artist.

Our day-to-day functions also have the environment in mind, incorporating details such as local herbal teas, low-flow water taps, recycled toilet paper and perishables, eco-friendly washing powders and cleaning products, and biodegradable packaging.

What does a better world mean to you?

Open, transparent and authentic communication.

What would be your biggest sacrifice in running a small business?

Cooking and baking - unfortunately I don't have much time for either.

Who's your biggest inspiration?

My children. They inspire me every day to be present.

Do you live by any mantra?

Comparison is suffering.

What does success mean to you?

Being surrounded by people you love: at work, at home and having the freedom to pursue things that light you up.

In the world of environmental sustainability, what's an innovative company you'd recommend and why?

Patagonia. They believe our environment is under threat of extinction and aim to use their resources, their brand, their voice to do what they can to create change. Bold moves such as a genuine attempt to produce less and slow growth by repairing existing garments and educating their audience on more sustainable options has created a brand that was built on an authentic base, prior to sustainability becoming a trend. They're a real lesson in moving with your heart and passion to do good.

Where do you hope to be five years from now?

In the same place I am now, just with a little more free time.

ACKNOWLEDGEMENTS

First and foremost, thank you to my husband James. Your relentless support throughout this journey, from idea to time spent travelling, months of writing and moments of self-doubt, is everything. Your love and patience goes beyond measure, and without you, so much of what I do wouldn't be possible.

Thank you to Beatnik Publishing for helping me bring this publication to life, for your creative freedom and support.

To my multitalented photographer Erin; my sounding board, friend and so often my right hand. From working in kitchens together to travelling countries in one another's pocket, we've come so far. Thank you for taking a chance on me, and this project. Thank you for your patience while I try to describe what brightness or tones mean to me in a colour grade, or while I'm trying to find a viable lunch option. Thank you for your kind and generous soul, for endless deep and puzzling conversations on long car rides, late into the night, over the phone or with cups of tea in hand, and of course your immense talent and the beauty you've brought to this publication.

Thank you to all of the business owners within these pages - for your time, your generosity and all that you do for your community and our world. It was an absolute honour getting to know you and sharing your stories.

And thank you, the reader. It's hard to explain the amount of work that goes into a book, any book. But I hope you find inspiration, empathy and understanding, wisdom, motivation, love, positivity and growth from these pages for your own journey forward.

GIVING BACK

This book is about exploring a new way of being. One that we as a society not only should, but must do, in order to protect our future. Although perfection is unattainable we must find ways to become better in our pursuits and have faith that every action we take, big or small, contributes to a more positive result.

For me this book became a journey through these notions and an ode to this cause. In light of this to lessen our impact as much as possible environmentally this book has been printed mindfully on FSC paper with vegetable inks in small batches. The kilometres clocked on our road trip have been paid back to worthy offsetting programmes to become climate neutral.

PUBLISHER'S NOTE

Beatnik Publishing works with sustainability in mind. In a business sector that has generally had a very high carbon footprint we actively take steps to minimise ours. We are a small team with minimal overheads. Our books are printed using FSC (sustainably sourced) paper. The inks used in the production of this book are vegetable based. We are mindful of not creating waste, and we try to plan our print runs to avoid the unnecessary disposal of unsold books. For Wild Kinship we wanted to go further so have purchased carbon credits through Climatecare.org to offset the emissions created in the shipping (by sea) of the books from our printer.

We still believe the printed book has a place in the modern world, but ask you to treasure it, lend it and value it for the combined effort that has gone into its creation.

ABOUT THE PHOTOGRAPHER

Erin Cave is a naturopath and portraiture, lifestyle and product photographer based in Mount Maunganui. Her love for photography comprises of being able to capture tiny moments of reality that stay forever unchanged and showcase beautiful everyday mundanities. She's passionate about naturopathy, herbalism, recipe curation and creating a kinder, healthier world.

ABOUT THE AUTHOR

Monique Hemmingson is a writer and avid wellness advocate for our planet, mind and body. As a former whole foods café owner, Monique became inspired by the range of forward-thinking, conscious small business models she'd come in contact with during this venture and realised they had an important story to tell and offering to communicate with the world.

Monique lives in Papamoa Beach with her husband James, their daughter Lulu Bloom and dog Remy. She's passionate about travel, design, whole foods, holistic wellness and creative entrepreneurship.

"You cannot get through a single day without having an impact on the world around you. What you do makes a difference, and you have to decide what kind of difference you want to make."

Jane Goodall